STOUR SEASONS

RONALD BLYTHE

CANTERBURY
PRESS
Norwich

© Ronald Blythe 2016

First published in 2016 by the Canterbury Press Norwich
Editorial office
3rd Floor, Invicta House,
108–114 Golden Lane,
London EC1Y 0TG

Canterbury Press is an imprint of Hymns Ancient & Modern Ltd
(a registered charity)
13A Hellesdon Park Road, Norwich,
Norfolk, NR6 5DR, UK

www.canterburypress.co.uk

Acknowledgement is made for the extract from
T. S. Eliot: 'Ash Wednesday', Part IV, in
Collected Poems 1909–1962, Faber & Faber, 2002.

British Library Cataloguing in Publication data

A catalogue record for this book is available
from the British Library

978 1 84825 884 6

Typeset by Mary Matthews
Printed and bound in Great Britain by CPI Group (UK) Ltd

Contents

Contents

Contents

ALSO BY RONALD BLYTHE

The Wormingford Series

Word from Wormingford
Out of the Valley
Borderland
A Year at Bottengoms Farm
The Bookman's Tale
River Diary
Under a Broad Sky
Village Hours
In the Artist's Garden
Stour Seasons

Fiction

A Treasonable Growth
Immediate Possession
The Short Stories of Ronald Blythe
The Assassin

Non-Fiction

The Age of Illusion
William Hazlitt: Selected Writings
Akenfield
The View in Winter
Writing in a War
Places: An Anthology of Britain
From the Headlands
Divine Landscapes
Private Words
Aldeburgh Anthology
Going to Meet George
Talking about John Clare
First Friends
The Circling Year
Field Work
Outsiders: A Book of Garden Friends
At Helpston

At the Yeoman's House

JANUARY

Wormingford Mere

ANOTHER year, and cause for meditation. What better than to sit in the new armchair and to watch the seagulls circling. And to think. Although this is a grand term for what is going on in my head at 6 a.m. It is still dark, and it takes another hour before the bare fields and trees take shape. Not a resolution in sight. Instead, a kind of freedom. Another year in which to do what I like – which is to work hard and idle hard. You need to be gifted to do nothing.

An old neighbour who is younger than me has gone to God. He liked going to Scotland. I take his funeral. Barry tolls him on his way. We sing 'Immortal, invisible', the ancient church filled to the doors, the pale winter light infiltrating the arches. The service sheet says '72'. A strong man, they said. The hymn, in a magical last burst, speaks of light's hiding God.

The young undertaker takes me on a meandering walk through the memorials to the new grave, where I wait for the mourners to catch up. How often has this happened in a thousand years. Then off to the Beehive pub, the cars crawling through the dank lane. Rooks circling now. The wind getting up.

We have a mere. Not every parish can say this. It is, of course, mysterious and legendary. A stork is more likely to rise in it than a sword. Pike take comfort in its black mud. Ages ago, we cooked a pike in a fish-kettle. Not an exciting dish. More

1

like eating an enormous pin-cushion, spitting bones all the way. And too spiky to offer to the cat, who sat at our feet with imploring eyes. But it was a great event, catching and cooking a pike. Poor creature. It might just as well have lived another hundred years in the lonely mere, propagating legends.

Meres were licensed for suicide: bad lots, betrayed girls, the usual thing. Plots for Thomas Hardy – not for natural history. We are very watery. Streams, ponds, wet places, the lovely Stour itself, keep up a perpetual glitter and sound. Although the mere itself maintains its old silence. It is broken only when the birds rise in a startled flash and clatter.

A general patching-up after the gale is going on. Most spectacular was the abseiler at Little Horkesley, who swung around the damaged tower on the rope, saving us millions from the scaffolders. Some old churches have 'put holes' in their towers: small built-in places where the flint might be extracted in order that a temporary pole might be put in place and staging erected.

When looking at church architecture, always start outside. Walk around the building to get the hang of it. This is what I was advised to do when I was twelve, and have done ever since. All the same, the opening of the door for the first time can be only a little less exciting than opening the pyramid. And that smell of vases and hymn books, robes, and sanctity. How it hits you! And the graffiti, the 'I was here' statement in an uncertain hand.

We use our fine hearse as a bookstall. It has shining painted wheels, and while not exactly a chariot of fire, it must have given panache to a funeral. I can imagine it crackling over the gravel.

But here I am, at the beginning of the year, walking ahead of its first loss, and saying: 'He cometh up, and is cut down, like a flower . . .'

John Bottengoms 1375

WALKING with Mother long ago, lopping the heads off flowers as we went, I was told what a pity it was to have given birth to such an unkind boy. As Mary and I drove to church, we slowed down to see a fine patch of snapdragon in Barn Hall Lane. Why didn't I join the Wild Flower Society? she said. This I did, and became immensely learned. Only the learning, like the snapdragon (*Linaria vulgaris*), stays patchy.

A few years ago, I listed all the plants that grew on the once 70 acres of Bottengoms Farm, walking them before breakfast and after supper, and carrying a notebook. It was the time of set-aside, when fields went untouched for three years; so I hoped I would find some ancient flower from the Middle Ages. But all I discovered was what used to be called the aftermath – the growth that softened and coloured the land after harvest. Poppies, pimpernels.

The Wild Flower Society sent me its register. Yesterday, mid-January, I found that primroses at Bottengoms bloom all the year round, that catkins are showing in the track, that the grass is sodden in a kind of livid green, and that the hellebores (Christmas rose), both white and pink, need to have their muddy leaves clipped for their full glory to be manifest.

Pottering about in the winter warmth, I prayed for the flooded, for New Yorkers, for those without winter flowers – botanical and spiritual. 'You are sheltered down here,' visitors say.

There was a John Bottengoms who perished in 1375. I see him taking shelter from the cold – the plague, maybe – judging the weeds, crossing himself as he prays to St Benedict (12 January), plodding two miles to mass, bothered by purgatory, envying his betters their ability to pay for a short stay in it.

As one grows old, aspects of belief wither and fall away like petals, leaving a stout centre. Prayer becomes Herbertian, 'something understood', and not a religious bothering. Best of all is holy quietness. And then there is gratitude. To have got this far!

Benedict for January. He did wonders in the north, until the last three years made him an invalid. His faith and his creativity wore him out. But what a life! A librarian, a singer, a builder, a traveller, gifted with restlessness and inspired by Christ, he perished in winter, leaving behind him a wonderful warmth. He taught Bede, the first known writer of English prose – and, they said, a light of the Church. Bede is also the only Englishman in Dante. Benedict would have applauded.

When I read these old writer-saints, I hear music in snowstorms. I feel that they would have been uncomfortable with my present winter – and horrified by my central heating. As for the new radiators in Little Horkesley Church, words would fail them. My Georgian ancestors in Suffolk put straw in their box pews, and fastened themselves in for long sermons.

The parson in his lofty pulpit stared down. There they were, his flock. There stood he, their shepherd. Breath floated around the church when they sang – possibly a hymn by Bede which hadn't got lost. 'Sing we triumphant hymns of praise.' But more likely slow, droning psalms.

An old neighbour, now with God, lacked patience with those who expected to be warm in church – 'Put more clothes on!' Archaeology reveals arthritic bones in the monastery garden. Some years ago, I discovered a fitted carpet round a Tudor font.

Bishop Heber and the Buddha

I AM reading Montaigne. My ivory tower is a square Tudor room that stares east. Low-ceilinged, clogged with books, it is where I am happiest. The spring-in-winter days breed roses.

They look through the window. I look out at the steep hill. The quietness rather than the silence is a kind of bliss. The white cat has to be lifted off papers.

Epiphany is both within and abroad. Poor Paul is involuntarily encased in another room, one with little light. Writing to the Ephesians, he tells them that he has broken through the limits of his Jewish faith in order to 'preach the unsearchable riches of Christ to the Gentiles'. Had Paul not been locked up, he would have done this in some Roman theatre or marketplace, not in letters. Bunyan would not have written had they let him preach. We find ourselves in small rooms.

And there are these once-a-year venues, the New Year's party rooms in the surrounding villages where we steer our way through the people we meet most weeks to those we meet annually. Logs blaze, small children find their way through a forest of legs, dogs are not too pleased, and, although it is almost warm enough to sit on the terrace, we hug glasses of mulled wine.

Driving home in his car, the Colonel repeats how fortunate we are to live here among true friends, and I am a boy again on my bike. Or a youthful historian, searching out the 1630s, when John Winthrop took a shipload of East Anglians to Massachusetts via these very same lanes.

Their luggage included feather beds and seed corn. The latter, not being clean, brought our wildflowers to New England. But here are their abandoned farmhouses and wool-weaving villages, still standing in unlikely perfection among the empty onion and sugar-beet fields, the low wheat, the gaunt January trees, and in the yellow afternoon light.

When I take matins in one of their abandoned churches, we sing Reginald Heber's 'Brightest and best of the sons of the morning'. This lovely Epiphany hymn was written in one of the Bishop's children's exercise books. To his wonderment, he heard it sung on St Stephen's Day in Meerut, in India.

He wrote: 'It is a remarkable thing, that one of the earliest, the largest, and handsomest churches in India, as well as one of the best organs, should be found in so remote a situation, and in sight of the Himalaya mountains.'

I preached on the youthful Buddha, as well as Christ 'going forth'. And, although January, there was this April light and softness, and no doubt a sea of snowdrops in the wood below the churchyard. We should have looked. At the service, a walker with his backpack and stick beside him in the pew, and now on his way.

Roger and I had Sunday lunch in our pub: roast beef, Yorkshire pudding, beer. Comfort. But the worship haunted us, the Epiphany language, the singing. 'Richer by far is the heart's adoration.' Heber had been thinking of the Olney hymns when he wrote his own. India got into them.

There are degrees of daylight, just as there are degrees of enlightenment. Think about them all, I say. They are journeys. The word 'journey' comes from 'as far as one can walk in a day'. Seagulls have arrived inland. They fly low, searching, screeching, their whiteness turning black.

The Still, Small Voice

HAVING wheeled barrow-loads of mulch from the so-called back lawn – a rich kingdom for snowdrops – so that the mower can have its way, I begin to shape the summer. Snowdrops and snowflakes for Candlemas onwards, and both for the feast of the Purification.

It is a mild, bright January afternoon, and the horses opposite break into little gallops every now and then. Yesterday, all three parishes ate great piles of food in the old village school, where above our talk I could hear the chanting of the alphabet and the seven times table, the stamping of winter

6

boots, and the singing of the morning assembly hymn.

At today's weddings and funerals, those under 50 embark on them with much uncertainty. Now and then I go to Robert Louis Stevenson for prayers – those that he wrote to his Samoan household. I imagine his Edinburgh accent becoming fainter and fainter as his tuberculosis fed on him.

His widow said: 'With my husband, prayer, the direct appeal, was a necessity. He was happy to offer thanks for that undeserved joy, when in sorrow or pain, to call for strength to bear what must be borne.'

I don't know about undeserved joy. Like grace, joy is there for the taking. We all deserve a bit of it, and if we miss it, it is mostly our own fault. Mrs Stevenson said: 'After all work and meals were finished, the pu, or war conch, was sounded from the back veranda and the front, so that it might be heard by all. I don't think it ever occurred to us that there was any incongruity in the use of the war conch for the peaceful invitation to prayer.'

I found Stevenson's little book in a tumbledown shop where a big dog lived. An unattended bookshop on the other side of the road was filled with treasures, and customers dodged the traffic to buy them. Then another copy arrived; so they sit together with my sermons, and Samoa and the Stour Valley make common prayer.

Long ago, when our faith was young, the Epiphany was celebrated as Christ's baptismal time. Four hundred years later, it became the feast of the Manifestation of Jesus as the Christ or redeemer of the Gentiles. A flood of divine light poured through the universe to make him plain to us. St Paul found it all rather a puzzle, this light which lightened every man. This light that began as a star, and continues to illuminate everything we do or say.

And then there are the words that Thomas Hardy loved more than anything else in the Bible, and which are written on his memorial window in Stinsford Parish Church. He

7

was probably flinching from noisy preaching and the pulpit generally when he heard that the Lord was not in the wind or in the earthquake or the fire, but in the still small voice.

It is often in silence that God speaks to us. At the same time, we must not hide away like Elijah in a cave, but stand on a mountain top. Listening is a very grown-up thing to do. To be a good listener is wonderful. Poets and novelists have their ear to the ground – and to the skies. And maybe especially at the Epiphany illumination of so many mysteries. During it, we read one of the most beautiful of all stories, a boy being called by his name, Samuel, by his God.

Gustav Holst and Martin Shaw

MARKET DAY. The village bus twists and turns through the lanes. On it are old folk, students, workmen, the woman who reads paperbacks all the way. There is an Italianate villa where the naval rating who helped to bury Rupert Brooke *en route* to Gallipoli lived; there is the hill where Martin Shaw composed 'Hills of the North, rejoice'. And there, across the liquid landscape, is the little house where my aunt spent her life making lace for the altar.

But, in the market town, the stone griffins on the church tower maintain their watch, seeing off goblins and foul fiends. I sense a new feeling of things not being as prosperous as they were. And, as always, faces from boyhood appear in the old street – not phantom features, but young faces grown old along with my own, especially in Waitrose.

The Epiphany proceeds. The Queen joins the Three Kings in the Chapel Royal; and in our three ancient parishes we sing and pray the journeying liturgy. Soon, we will be walking into Lent. Last midnight I wandered around the garden, staring at stars, and followed by the white cat. Stansted planes flew silently through golden clouds. An extra quietness prevailed. Snow was out of the question, and winter was no more than a name. But I checked the oil tank, and it answered with a half-full clunk.

Then came the clearing of desks for this year's work. Only not quite yet. Let January get into its stride. Hear some music. Answer letters. Remember that Keith is coming to decorate John Nash's studio, now my bedroom. He went to it every day at ten o'clock, and came down from it at four o'clock. His easel fronted a north light, and there was a single 40-watt bulb to encourage it. We never entered without permission, and he never left it without a kind of sadness. It was never swept or dusted, and cocoa-tin lids piled with ash were rarely emptied.

When he went away to fill up the sketchbooks, he cleared a space for me in which to write. But I never worked in his studio with its north light and half-light, but always in the sunshine. His pupils would enter this room with reverence, looking forward to the time when they, too, would attain its murk and hereditary litter and spiders' webs. For it takes an age to create one's own peerless dust and muddle.

I was once told the tale of Gustav Holst's reaction to the new composing room which his wife made ready for him when he was away. Glorious it was, with great windows on to the beautiful Thaxted countryside. But they said that he never wrote a note in it, and sat by the hearth in his old house, as he always did. His suite *The Planets* might soar to the skies, but it was created by the hearth.

Benjamin Britten worked in a window which faced the sea, and which at times was sprayed with it. But the local stationer sold postcards of the window, and, when visitors to Aldeburgh stood on the sea wall to watch him, he had to find a hiding place.

William Hazlitt, the great essayist who longed to be an artist, insisted that no one should approach an artist at work – that something sacred was happening at that moment. I once read 'Kubla Khan' in the room where Coleridge had written it, rocking his baby son to sleep at the same time. Nash walked to his studio in my room every day.

Secret Ministries

THE weatherman proclaims an amazing sunrise. I cannot recall him saying this before. At the moment, the window frames total darkness. It is 6 a.m. Not a person to miss a touch of glory, however, I keep my eye on the outside. A Stansted-bound plane hovers in view, moving like the Epiphany star, brightly, deliberately, to its rightful destination. Then an even darker darkness. It will be a long time before the promised splendour.

There is a slight frost. Not at all like the one in Coleridge's poem. He is in his 20s, in the cottage at Nether Stowey. It is glory time, too. His wife has gone to bed. The fire in the grate is no more than a flutter. He rocks the cradle and promises his baby son a glorious life. Outside:

> The frost performs its secret ministry
> Unhelped by any wind . . .
> The inmates of my cottage, all at rest,
> Have left me to that solitude, which suits
> Abstruser musings . . .

Long ago, I sat in that same room, stilled by its confusion of privacy and fame as the youthful father's eyes turned from his child to his page. I now wait for the sunrise in an older, larger room that faces due east. Some say that the old people preferred to live in this direction as disease came from the south. Possibly it was because the wells and ponds were polluted by the summer heat. Or it could have been a religious thing. We still lie east to west in our graves.

Gradually, taking its time, reminding itself that it is Phoebus making his entrance, the sun comes up over the barn, a truly fantastic sight, all golden lances and display, shooting radiance everywhere. And at 8 a.m. precisely. It throws everything before it into silhouette.

As this house creaks in the intense cold, Coleridge promises his son a country life for all seasons – one where God is 'the Great Universal Teacher'. Outside my ancient farmhouse, the scene quietens down, as it were. Gold becomes yellow; black grows green; shadows become familiar objects.

My Epiphany sermons take in the Dark Ages, which, as we now know, were not dark at all. Think of the light of Sutton Hoo. But, before Christ, there was this melancholy, this northern-Europe fatalism, this lack of conviction that the spring and summer would return. This acceptance of Valhalla as a mead hall in which only the brave in this life had entrance.

The theme brought me back to the naming of England, where eventually the raiders would settle, grow corn, follow a star. They were called Angles because they came from an angle-shaped province in Germany. Angle-land became England. Except here, where both dawn and sunsets are part of a unique climate of what is still called East Anglia.

Another little boy lies sleeping, as intellectuals as well as ordinary folk peer down at him. A young clergyman writes an Epiphany hymn in his son's exercise-book. It is 'Brightest and best of the sons of the morning'.

FEBRUARY

Timothy in Winter

WINTER made a brief appearance, like a minor character in an old play. It whitened the edges of things, and, having arrived, was very still. Nothing moved. I could have picked some flowers – white periwinkle, daisies, a rose or two, pussy willow. Snowberries clung to the thicket by the horse pond. Birds pretended to starve. There was a thin skin of ice on the puddles, like the cracked surface of brouillés.

I walked up the track to visit a hedgerow oak of awe-inspiring years, to regard it and wonder at it. When it was a youth, *circa* Charles I possibly, it had been made to surrender wood for a carpenter, which caused it to twin. Thus two vast trees from the same stock have been seeing the centuries out since goodness knows when.

Long ago, Bud the roadman would knock on the door with: 'I thought I would give you a look.' He could not read or write, with the result that he knew things that I could never know. Mystery and wonder invaded his dark face. 'Well there,' he would conclude, 'that's what they say.' We drank homemade wine. Then: 'I must get going.' His bike would crackle on the gravel.

If it was summer, the tremendous oaks on Maypole Hill would become models of tree stillness. This was at another house, and at another time. We each carry such fragmentary experiences around with us, sharp and bright as icicles.

Timothy, the lectionary says. He was Paul's youthful bishop. 'Only Luke is with me,' the old man complains. 'The cloke that I left at Troas with Carpus, when thou comest, bring with thee, and the books, *but especially the parchments.*' How the years drop away when I read this.

Timothy was the son of a mixed marriage between a Jewess and a heathen – i.e. from a pagan village, or a countryman who worshipped rural gods. Paul sent him to confirm the Christians at Corinth and Thessaly in the faith. Their relationship is vivid, one of teacher and pupil, pastor and lamb. They changed the world. Thus Timothy for before Lent, the young star on the move.

I like to think that the Quakers had their Timothy in the form of James Parnell. His Paul was George Fox. Parnell, in his teens, walked all the way from Retford to Carlisle prison to be his pupil – his 'bishop', no less. Fox himself had climbed Pendle Hill in Lancashire, where he listened to – silence. Thus the quiet ministry of the Society of Friends was created.

Poor young Parnell was not quiet when he returned to the Suffolk–Essex border. He stood outside parish churches as the congregation emerged and 'disturbed the peace'. But there was no peace, only religious rants and the like. His talk-in-Christ was a kind of poetry, but this was not wanted. So they put him in Colchester prison, where the gaoler's wife turned him into a sideshow, eventually murdering him.

From my boyhood on, I have paused at his cell. It is an open brick fireplace, high up in the wall, from which he fell while being exhibited. He would have been the perfect subject for a Britten opera, I used to think. Parnell, the silencer of religious noise. Did he take Fox a warm coat and something to read?

One of the Coldest Times Ever

AGES ago, when I was beginning to write, I put up a bravura defence of winter. 'Winter wild, and winter drear, Surely wintertime is here,' we sang as children. I didn't believe it. Snow elated me. Black-ice ponds thrilled me. Thus, when I listened to the beginnings of the present blanket condemnation of winter by the weathermen, I was genuinely puzzled.

My defence of it was in a youthful 'literary middle', as I believe such thousand-word essays were called in *The Observer*. It was headed 'A good word for winter'. These provocative opinions, sharp and short, were in the tradition of William Hazlitt, the British Montaigne.

Sitting with my back to the hot sun as it blazes through the study window, and with boys and girls and frantic dogs tobogganing on the steep field, I find myself thinking that it would not go amiss for the young forecaster in his smart suit to point out what an indescribably beautiful day it has been. Of course, less so if one is on the road or on the train, when winter can be an inconvenient, or even dangerous loveliness. All the same, its 'dreariness' these days is usually more on the screen than outside.

And why do most seventeenth-century artists have everyone outside when it snows? This was one of the coldest times ever, as we know. For one thing, it was warmer than in the house. Just look at the unglazed windows, the rocking shutters, the miserable thread of smoke winding up into the blue from the hefty chimneys. Then see the frantic exercise outside. You can almost hear the shouts, the barks, the pleasure.

Such sounds were duplicated on my hill. It was Sunday, but no church, which made the day somehow unlicensed and strange, it being impossible to get up the farm track. It was deep in drifts, scribbled all over by bird feet and rabbit paws. And here was a fine something-before-Lent sermon lying unspoken

14

on the table. And then I find that it is Septuagesima in the old language, when 'we may be mercifully delivered by thy goodness, for the glory of thy name'. When Henry, the Vicar, rings up at seven in the morning to say, 'No services today', for who could slide to church on such icy lanes? I reply that we must say our prayers at home. Yet it is odd, winter or no winter.

The first icicle of the season jabs from the guttering, a kind of black-white spike pointing to the earth. I scoop snow from a trough and scatter 'wild bird seed', which is what it says on the label. There now, I tell myself, I have done my bit. I have shown true regret for not taking matins, and I have fed the hungry. And I am enjoying, at long range, the happiness of the season. And the white cat on the sill wears a nimbus of snowy sunshine, and wisely declines an invitation to go out.

In Good King Charles's winter days, even the court joined the sliders on the Thames. The river was almost solid ice, and people lit bonfires on it, built temporary shops on it, skated to the sea or to Oxford on it. The big thing was to roast an ox on it. Many people in villages or towns perished from the cold, of course. They were called the poor. Many people, young and old, were exhilarated by the sharpness of life, not death. Walk carefully. See the briefly transformed view. And, as the Revd Sydney Smith advised, 'Keep good fires.'

Galilee, O Galilee

OLD friends in an old bedroom, having an old conversation. Thin snow outside. It is St Valentine's Day, and the Pope is resigning. Fancy that. 'But why not?' we say, knowing nothing about it. How weary he looks. Weariness is something we understand.

Hyacinths topple and sway like censers, but we maintain

our equilibrium. This ancient house stares east into a partly
blocked view; for we dwell in the 'Suffolk–Essex highlands',
an unexpected countryside to most people. Snowy news-
papers, snowy sheets. The housekeeper enters with milky
coffee. Holy pictures on the walls. Then home through the
churned-up mud to Bottengoms, and a further extension of the
same territory.

I am judging a children's poetry competition for St
Edmundsbury Cathedral. Pre-puberty poets are best. On the
radio, the Poet Laureate holds forth on the Song of Solomon.
Apparently, they thought twice about including this ravishing
work in the canon. How glad we are that they did. The white cat
sleeps on the cooker.

After lunch, I brave the winds, and cut a drain so that the
water in the track can run freely. A green woodpecker comes to
have a drink. Should a walker have passed, I would have said:
'Spring will soon be here,' or something equally brilliant, but
no one comes. I rake until I cannot see. Then I go back to the
poetry competition to balance the pros and cons, as a judge
must. It is a solemn thing to sit in judgement.

Jean's horses tumble about beneath the catkin hedge to
keep warm. The snow becomes a brief blizzard. All this on
St Valentine's Day. My archaeologist neighbour calls to say
that they are digging by the river – by the ring burials – and
I imagine our slender ancestors chipping away at flints, and
singing, maybe.

Quinquagesima has come and gone, the day they buried
George Herbert. I choose his version of the 23rd Psalm for my
Lent One. I hear his lute. One's religious memory has a way of
retaining things that our mature beliefs can find embarrassing,
or of great value, if inexplicable. At Sunday school, I faced a
long framed text whose words have become lost, but whose
background – a picture of boats sailing on Galilee – remains

thrilling to this day. Although, even then, I knew that as art it was terrible.

Not like the medieval wall-painting in Wiston Church, below Bottengoms, in which this same scene takes place with masterly conviction. And yet, at the same time, with no great meaning. And how hard it is to get the doggerel choruses of infancy out of one's head. Memory is both a ragbag and a treasure house. It doesn't know the meaning of taste.

I remember going to D. H. Lawrence's Eastwood, and seeing the then dilapidated chapel where he attended Sunday school, and in which he had sung 'Galilee, sweet Galilee, where Jesus loved so much to be' and how these words and their tune would stay unforgettable, although it was easy to rid himself of Christianity.

Paul suffered dreadfully from not being able to forget Saul. His mind had been trained to contain both the best and the worst. An honest memory is the only asset we possess that can show us the self that God recognizes. The Epiphany exposes us, as well as enlightens us. Sundials say 'I tell only the sunny hours' because it is all that they can do. Given half a chance, our memories would do the same. But life would not be half as interesting.

Constable's Country

'I THINK I could turn and live with animals, they are so placid and self-contained,' the American poet Walt Whitman wrote. And placid was a word for the English countryside which John Constable loved.

Having seen it in riot when the farmworkers rose against their starvation wages, with rick-burnings and protest, he looked back at the peaceful Suffolk scenes of his boyhood when they were called peasants, and there seemed to be a God-given order between the classes.

Some years ago, when I was staying with my brother in New South Wales, we drove along the shore of Botany Bay, and we spoke of all the poor people, men and women, who had been shipped there from our own Suffolk world on the hulks that had brought African slaves to Bristol. Such journeys were equivalent to a flight to the moon.

Meanwhile, on my right in the plane sat a fault-finding woman for whom nothing was right. 'Isn't it amazing that we can now cross the world in a day,' I said. She looked at me as if she was about to report a lunatic. So I went on reading Barbara Pym, and looking out of the window. What she wanted was an ally, but I sank myself in the passing clouds, and said no more.

Literature is filled with dreaded fellow-travellers. Now and then they are prophetic. Returning to London from Suffolk, John Constable said, 'How do you do?' to the person sitting opposite, remarking on the beauty of the countryside, who answered, 'Yes, sir. We call it the Constable country.'

On the whole, I like looking out of the window in trains, especially *en route* to Cornwall, which once took five enchanted hours from Paddington. Or *en route* to Edinburgh, looking up especially at Durham on its mighty rock, and then across the sands to Lindisfarne, seeing saints all the way.

Walkers past my farmhouse are quite an event, and a human voice is a rarity. But the great trees – ashes, chestnuts, fruit trees – are already beginning to sound with birds. February is upon them, a miserable month in books, but far from it during our current seasons.

The trouble with those popular poems of the seasons is that they no longer say what is happening *now*. Certainly, almost none of the traditional tasks. In fact, living in what must have been for hundreds of years a 'tay', or 'tigh' (Suffolk–Essex border language for some stranded farm), I often feel the landscape itself asking to be ploughed and sown when the green tips are a mere hint on the trees.

But the bulbs are up, thousands of them, and have certainly gone forth and multiplied. So now there has to be the last great clear-up, the final raking of the grass, the first tidying of the beds, the noting of the dead among the living, and, best of all, the promise ahead.

Unimaginably, Lent is in the offing. Sometimes, I think how relaxing it would be to live near a cathedral, and to have the Church's year all worked out, beautifully and professionally, and laid before me, although our parish magazines present each village with its distinct personality and liturgy almost miraculously, and fine creatures as well as fine folk are liveable-with in all three.

'Where am I on Sunday?' I sometimes ask. Where, indeed? At this moment, having held back for as long as it dare, the sleet rattles down in frozen rain-rods.

Getting About

NATURE'S light is tentative and subdued. Wild waves have driven the gulls inland. They bounce around on the muddy field, gorging on horse-feed. Not a soul about, and almost painfully quiet.

I choose hymns for matins and evensong, and rewrite a sermon. For there comes a moment when, if it is not blasphemous to say so, I have written what I have written. When nothing should be added.

'Just imagine', I tell myself, 'how worrying it must have been for the infant Church to hear that it must accept the variety of human experience.' And particularly for Saul/Paul. Many of the first Christians belonged to a religion with set rules, but now, Saul says, you must leave its protection and follow the

19

teachings of Jesus with your own individual gifts – having first found out what they are.

The future saints would always be a nuisance to the Church, because they would either break its rules, or fail to understand them. But orthodoxy had its 'beauty of holiness', as the Epiphany tells us. And especially its journeys.

Talking of which, I went to London for the first time in ages. The commuter train lurched into Liverpool Street. Vicky came with me, and then we went our separate ways: she to see her weeks-old nephew, me to a vast literary lunch. Gales were promised, but not until we went home. The City streets were golden; the people, if not quite up to being Thomas Traherne's angels, a nice change from the Wormingford horses, fine though they are.

Home by the early evening. The white cat looked up – her only movement since I left. And the news of a ruined journey: one that I took every year, to Cornwall, taking care to sit on the left so as not to miss the dramatic sea at Dawlish as it hurled itself at the line. I was going to see the Cornish poets James Turner and Charles Causley. And to walk by myself on the headlands.

My first visit to Penzance was with Mother. We went to a vast Methodist church where the singing overwhelmed us. I can hear it still – just as I can see the Atlantic boiling against the granite. We would ring up to ask if it was fine at St Ives, then walk across from Land's End.

I love Thomas Hardy's Cornwall, with its terrifying cliffs and its unforgettable glimpses of his first wife at St Juliot. It is being cut off by floods, and a railway line going nowhere would have enthralled him. It amazes us, this washing away of the west. Although we did once go to the eight o'clock communion in a church that had been under water. 'They all came and swept it out,' the young priest explained. The congregation, he meant. We sang from a wet hymn-book.

But nature is changing. Our defences, our money, are a kind of impotence. They cut us down to size – or rather they tell us where and how to live. Some unknown farmer in Shakespeare's day raised my house a foot above the cart track to make it bone dry. Them dry bones. But the heartbreaking interiors when the water gets in! They need no words on the screen.

Blackbirds and linnets devour old cake below my window, itself due east, as the 'old people' insisted. Because of the resurrection. The sun was there to wake you up.

In the village, a mile or two away, the days are pulling out. It is what they say. And the Stour is high. And a few trees lie flat on their faces in the drenched fields. And the hellebores are out.

St Ambrose Sings

ST PAUL tells the Church to put on love as though it was a garment; to wear it so that the world can see it. As both a Jew and a Roman, he was entitled to wear the recognizable dress of both nationalities. In the same edict, he commands the followers of Jesus to 'Sing psalms and hymns and spiritual songs.'

There was a time when this order appeared to have been forgotten; it was then passionately restated by St Ambrose, the Bishop of Milan who had not been baptized when he was made a bishop by acclamation. His 'O Jesus, Lord of heavenly grace' was sung every Monday.

Ambrose is called the father of church music in Latin Christianity. St Augustine said: 'How greatly did I weep in your hymns and canticles, how moved I was by the voices of your sweet-speaking church! The voices flowed into my ears, and the truth was poured into my heart.' This singing was imitated by almost all of its congregations.

We accept eighteen Ambrosian hymns and four Ambrosian poems as authentic, but it was their combined sound and language that continued to add to make 'songs of praise' the only aspect of Christianity known to most people.

Some hymn-writers possess a special reverence for many of us – a devotion that we hold on to all our lives. When I was in my twenties, the poets R. N. Currey, James Turner and W. R. Rodgers, and I 'spoke' hymns in the big, cold East Anglian churches, usually without so much as a by your leave.

I was nineteen when I first heard the magnificent Methodist hymn-singing in Cornwall when, on a Saturday night, fishermen perched on the window sills of pubs to sing 'O for a closer walk with God', and St Bernard's passionate 'Jesu, the very thought of thee' – a hymn that, some believed, had helped to civilize the world.

George Herbert famously made little of his poems, and told his friend to burn them if they were no good. Sensibly, this friend had them printed by the best publisher in Cambridge.

'Our' local hymns are 'Hills of the North, rejoice' and 'My song is Love unknown' – the first set by Martin Shaw, and the second by John Ireland. Its author, a youthful curate in the seventeenth century, was deprived of his living, but still ended up as a dean. All that remains of his country church is a big stone and a wide view. My mother's favourite hymn was 'My glorious Victor, Prince Divine, Clasp these surrendered hands in thine.'

Hymns tumble in and out of the books, and *Hymns Ancient and Modern* (1861) was 'a task of much labour', the preface confesses, not to mention much copyright, much cutting, and, eventually, much popularity. An old friend, Alan Cudmore, is my authority on hymns. I also love Thomas Hardy's mention of them. Once, when his lovers were strolling past a Dorset church, they heard a new hymn being practised. It was 'Abide with me'.

The Salvation Army's all-conquering weapon was the band-led hymn. Unfortunately, there are hymn-book-makers who do not allow their ignorance of literature to stop them meddling with some great hymns.

The Jews' peerless hymn-book is Psalms: all 150 of them carry the singing through the heights and depths of human existence. It was sung through the Holocaust. It is a pastoral one, but it never dates, and it is Christ's own songbook. It is hard not to 'hear' him and his family singing from it.

George Herbert in Lent

ASH Wednesday, with rooks being blown about the sky any old how. The sky itself is dove-grey, with blotches of gold. So I read Joel, and should weep between the porch and the altar. As a compromise, I read the whole of George Herbert's *The Church-porch*, something I have not done before, and in which I have to be a youth again. But I grow older as the poem runs on, and soon I am Herbert's age, late 30s, and a Wiltshire Lent encloses me. So long ago.

But the chalk breaks through the landscape, and the cathedral spire gathers up the local meditation just as it does this minute. Herbert was very Lenten. So many things happened to him then: birth, marriage, death, and this long 'entrance' poem. Joel criticizes the ritual fast. We are to rend our hearts, not our garments, and to be 'taught how to behave ourselves in church'. To fast is to 'starve sin'. It is Herbert who adds these injunctions.

It's true, we cannot reach Christ's fortieth day;
Yet to go part of that religious way,
    Is better than to rest;
We cannot reach our Saviour's puritie;
Yet we are bid, be holy ev'n as he.
In both let's do our best.

Pages and pages of Lenten advice and commands. Yet they do not make me squirm. Somebody has to say these things; so why not our finest Christian poet? He is bewilderingly undated. Neither modern nor old. But he hands it out, as they say. Do this, do not do that. At the least, there is a Lenten etiquette; at the most, a cleansing of the religious palate.

The Vicar has told me not to forget that 'thou art dust'; but Herbert does not. As I pass through the church door on Ash Wednesday, he tells me to remember many other things that I am, and they are far from dusty. Otherwise, would he not have ordered me to 'Shine like the sunne in every corner'?

Herbert's Lent is a far cry from the one that would have rung out in some of his neighbouring churches when the curses of A Commination were cried. Spring cheers his fast.

Hark, how the birds do sing,
    And woods do ring.
All creatures have their joy: and
    man hath his.

Divide these joys if you can. 'Lent, did you say?' the horses opposite ask. And they dance about and roll on the muddy grass. 'Lent, did I hear you say?' the starlings repeat, and they flock in a kind of winged quadrille Nayland way. 'Lent?' asks the white cat, and she falls off the radiator into the Whiskas. 'Lent?' the garden says: 'When are you going to make a start?'

I seem to have left my Prayer Book in some vestry or other. The one I have found here tumbles about in my hand, which is how it opened at the Commination curses. It was given to John, it says, in November 1910, when he was 17. And he wore it thin in a country church in the Chilterns; but only I would know this now. For such is the history of devotion or use. It cracks the cover, muddles the pages, and leaves a Commination wide open.

But there are red, red rubrics, and, surprisingly, a letter from Winston Spencer Churchill – a non-faster if ever there was one. I close it to watch the morning birds wheel over the hill. And to think what more I can say at a Lenten matins.

The Young Prisoners

EACH morning, at about six, tea in hand, I sit for an hour looking out of the window, regular as clockwork. At first, there is nothing to see in winter, then shadowy shapes are 'laid in', as the artist who once lived here might put it. The window-framing of what was outside held a fascination for him. Especially when it snowed.

Christians used to have their window-songs: one for morning, one for bedtime. They say that George Herbert rose from his deathbed, seized his lute, and sang his morning window-song. My morning window-song is silent but tuneful, my being a 'morning person', and not very bright in the late evening, my metabolism tending to peter out. I take it as a great kindness on nature's part to come into view every day.

A long time ago, there was a natural-history essay competition that Richard Mabey, David Attenborough, John Fowles, and I were asked to judge. The prize was £500, and publication in *The Sunday Times*. It was to honour the memory of Kenneth Allsop.

One year, a brilliant entry arrived from Dartmoor Prison. It was about bird-watching through a barred window, and we had to get permission from the prison governor for the caged naturalist to get his prize.

Windows have a way of limiting what one sees and, at the same time, intensifying the vision. I always try to get a window-seat on a plane, and do not always pull the little blind down at night. Vast cities briefly glitter below me. Night and day are on each other's heels, as in Genesis. Better not stare at the wings of the plane. They are flimsy, even patched. The Victorians raised classroom windows so that boys and girls could not see out, and would thus concentrate on their lessons. Although delighting in stained glass, such as the wonderful 1950s window in Little Horkesley Church in our benefice, I love churches where trees wave to me through clear glazing.

Poor Henry Howard, Earl of Surrey, could hear tennis being played below his prison window. Not quite 30, Henry VIII had him executed for 'treason', a trumped-up charge for a wild genius who had quartered his arms with those of Edward the Confessor. Howard's immense gift to English literature was to invent blank verse, the patterns in which Shakespeare would write his plays.

Young Surrey lies in Framlingham Church, in a sublime tomb below tall windows. His window-song is a little collection of rueful poetry which I often take from the shelf to find him 'looking out' with clear youthful eyes at his world. It is a terrible thing for a state to silence its writers, to block out their views, as all twentieth-century tyrants did their best to do.

Renaissance artists like to give the Holy Family a room with a view. High above the group, there is often a glassless window filled with scenery. A nearby hill, a blue stream, a ploughman, some birds, somewhere for the Child to play.

Once, in Burgundy, we found a small hotel at night, went to bed, and awoke to a maid throwing the shutters wide to the vineyards below. No glass, just scenery and a warm wind, swallows and shouts, church bells and life. Bonjour, monsieur! A glorious awakening, indeed.

I still find getting up, and sitting down opposite my window, pretty good, as does the white cat. Together we look.

Art and Theology

LEAP year. The study window wide to the sun, the white cat upside down to its warmth, the nesting birds bouncing over the new grass. At St Edmundsbury, we are creating the Edmund Centre for Arts and Theology. Art and theology are indivisible, of course, but sometimes it is necessary to point out their unity. Liturgy is art. Prayer is high art.

The Lenten desert was hideously artless for Jesus. A barbaric experience. Perhaps, when it entered his head that a jump from the Temple dome would rescue him from the degradation of execution, the beauty of Herod's creation lit up the desert darkness, and art itself revealed its imperishable nature.

Tragically, at the same time, he knew that the Romans would not let a work of art inspire a national rebellion. That they would not allow one stone to stand upon another. The loveliness of the Temple, of Jerusalem itself, made him cry.

Art and theology has to be understood at all levels. To assume that their connection is generally comprehended is one way of demolishing the temple. A friend finds that he has one of those updated hymn-books in his London church, where a politically correct hand has improved Herbert, Cowper, Wesley, etc. Where the little ignorant foxes have nibbled their way through the inspired text. So what to do?

How strange it is that everything should be understood. That a common denominator should be the rule. Our village church sings Newman's 'Praise to the Holiest in the height' with praiseworthy obscurity, getting its tongue round the poetry, and, maybe, its head round the sense. Ancient Mrs Smith in the second pew there, 'What is a higher gift than grace?'

I have always enjoyed the clashes between the creative impulse and strict theology in scripture, between the Word and its imagery. It is where the artist, the poet, steps in, not to

27

say big business. St Paul, in his attack on the cult of Diana at Ephesus, threatened its thriving silversmiths and caused a riot. Was the golden calf beautiful, a work of art?

One of my favourite 'artist' stories in the Old Testament, because it describes the process of utility to art so accurately, is in Isaiah 44. He takes two craftsmen, a blacksmith and a carpenter, to task. As an essential part of society, they could lead us all astray; for, besides being craftsmen, they are apt to be artists. They have the power to make useful things into aesthetic things. They must remain utilitarian, and not make objects that are so wonderful that one wants to worship them.

God told Moses: 'Do not make graven images, because, if you do, you are bound to lend them some of my holiness (wholeness).' And yet Moses had glorious works of art in beaten gold, the cherubim with spreading wings and looking into each other's lovely faces, seated above the Ark.

Other than the silver statues of Diana, there are no images in the New Testament. Yet Christianity would only be a few years old when the face of Jesus would be painted on the catacomb walls, and his early worshippers would begin to picture his teachings in every church. One meaning of iconoclasm is to make a face unidentifiable.

A Victorian St Alban stands on our reredos, a young soldier in a kilt – unworshipped, but loved; far away in time, yet close. An artist made him, and kept him near.

MARCH

'Remember, thou art dust'

ASH WEDNESDAY: even Joel wails in the wilderness, 'Repent, repent!' The white cat slumbers on a paid bill, the sun hot on her breast. The horses converse under the bare may-tree. The garden is covered with flowers. The spring has come.

For T. S. Eliot, it was the Ash Wednesday of 1930 as he asked:

> Who walked between the violet and the violet
> Who walked between
> The various ranks of varied green
> Going in white and blue, in Mary's colour,
> Talking of trivial things . . .

Waiting for the funeral to begin, dressed in our robes under the vast arch, we talk of the sky-high builders of the church as they cling to the scaffold ropes, carving an angel here and there, or painting glass for the clerestory.

It is Stoke-by-Nayland, where, as boys, we climbed the tower to see if you could really see the sea; for this is what they said. The verger would holler, 'Come down, you young varmints!' But on and on we would go, round and round, until we hit the firmament on high.

The cortège arrives. It is Marjorie, dear, dear friend. Marjorie, who settled her husband down after he had taken the service with, 'Dear, you did well.' And a glass of sherry. And here she comes, hidden in lilies. Both departed and present. For that is what death does: it takes you away and leaves you here. For:

> Here are the years that walk between, bearing
> Away the fiddles and the flutes, restoring
> One who moves in the time between sleep and
> waking, wearing
> White light folded . . .

The doors of this church are worth a journey; for they are white light folded. Angels, archangels, and princes made silvery by the Suffolk air soar as we enter.

How odd it is to stand at the lectern and talk about Marjorie, who should have been cooking our lunch. I hear her in my head. She should have been saying, 'Dear, you did well.' But there it is, this going and staying.

From the corner of my eye, *en-passant*, I catch the tablet to Canon Clibbon, whose daughter read poetry for me at the literary society. Ash Wednesday, maybe. All this a long time ago, as Eliot said.

I read Joel, who interrupted the temple services with his passionate oratory, his white-light-folded words.

The garden waits, or rather it grows like mad. The birds sing. The grass waves. Spring is a green ocean racing on and on. Wordsworth's little daffodils gather under the nut trees. The mud in the track shines between flints. The priest will mark my brow with ashes from incinerated palms. Dust I am, and to dust I will return.

After the funeral, we talk about Omar Khayyám in the pub. He was good on dust. Rose dust, human dust, stardust. Starving before Lent, on account of two consecutive funerals, I devour the sandwiches and feel well and very much alive. As one does in the presence of the dead. It can be their final gift, their making us grateful for the sun.

Friendships

THE artists John and Christine Nash called their inner circle 'the dear ones' – not from any feeling of exclusivity, but of management. Over the years, they had taught and belonged to various art movements in East Anglia. They had taken a practical part in everything from the Wormingford Dramatic Society to the Aldeburgh Festival.

John Nash, too, had been a plantsman and a musician. Looking through the windows from which he would paint on a winter's day, using its glazing bars to line up a drawing or a watercolour, I see more or less the same scene that he saw: a palette-shaped flower bed, my far neighbour's hilly pasture, some bone-idle horses, and greening ash trees. No traffic, but Tom's little plane might saunter past like the aeroplane in a child's storybook, archaic yet up to date. Nothing happens, yet everything happens. The scene is restful, yet vital.

Alan, a friend from my boyhood, arrives. We don't talk about our past but of this present, topping up a few mutual experiences of old age. We love the old liturgy, of course, but really know very little about today's Church. It's a mistake to try to keep up with trends where prayer is concerned: it must try to cope with those horrors of the world which are always with us, as Jesus said they would be; yet it must acknowledge that there is truth in the newness of love every morning.

I sometimes try to imitate a Jewish friend who returns to his room after breakfast to say his prayers, only I say mine washing up. And sometimes in the garden. And particularly now that I have cleared the grass of sticks and black leaves and debris, and step gingerly between purple saffron and the tracks made by badgers, trying, as always, to make up my mind whether it should be a wild garden or a proper garden – one that doesn't attract concern about my age, and its being too much for me.

As far as I can tell, nothing is too much for me, although I rule out the annual farm walk. But don't I walk to fetch the milk? To fetch the post? To fetch anything? Many years ago, this would have been a house of endless errands, of children bred to fetch and carry. Of never going empty-handed.

But how many of them, over the centuries, wouldn't have been struggling down the stairs at this hour of the day to feed stock before feeding themselves. How many would have crept from their beds in this very room where a typewriter clicks.

A long time ago, two youths arrived to fix the telephone, and one of them said, wonderingly: 'Listen, Tony. A typewriter!' – a then rare Olympia. The parish, the diocese, the Church, print a library every day. And to think there was a time when it took a week or a month to draw a capital letter.

Outside, everything is energized – including myself. But also free. Even the silvery Saviour and his angels and apostles, carved on the church doors at Stoke-by-Nayland by some contemporary of Chaucer, have a spring glitter.

George Herbert was strict when it came to opening a church door. At Bemerton, we open the same door as he opened, and we drink from the cup from which he drank. At Wormingford, we step down into the interior, each worshipper letting a little of the spring in, a fragment of birdsong which joins our psalms.

'When lilacs last in the dooryard bloomed'

A PAIR of jays, dressed to the nines, swing warily from the holly bush – although the whole village knows that the white cat has never caught a thing in her life, being sloth incarnate. Yet the fine birds look down on my feast of crusts and old Christmas nuts with caution. The day is still, its light subdued. We have to read Jeremiah and John, both good authors.

At the Suffolk Poetry Society meeting we listened to an American woman reading from Walt Whitman's 'Leaves of Grass'. President Lincoln has been assassinated in the theatre, but the violence has been contained, and somehow robbed of its lasting evil. The quiet New England voice says: 'When lilacs last in the dooryard bloom'd . . . I mourn'd, and yet shall mourn with ever-returning spring.' It is one of those openings which capture the imagination.

The Connecticut reader asks: 'Have you been to Connecticut?'

'Yes, but long ago. Though not in the fall.'

When Lincoln's coffin continues on its way, it might well have been down my farm track:

Amid lanes and through old
woods, where lately the violets
peep'd from the ground,
spotting the gray debris,
Amid the grass in the fields each
side of the lanes, passing the
endless grass,
Passing the yellow-spear'd wheat,
every grain from its shroud in
the dark-brown fields uprisen . . .

When the Suffolk farmers emigrated to New England in the seventeenth century, they took their seed corn with them, plus the seed of our wildflowers – or weeds, as we call them. Heartbreaking, it must have been. Did lilacs go, too? In order to bloom for a murdered president?

33

I tidy paths in warm sunshine. All the birds sing. Dutifully, I read Jeremiah and John, seeing what they have to say. Jeremiah despairs at our incorrigible nature: 'Can the leopard change his spots?' John records Jesus saying: 'I am the light of the world.'

It is Lent 4. Geese scream over to the river. Neighbours walk by. We tell each other the obvious: that the afternoon is warm and wonderful, that it is good to be out. In the evening, I read Kilvert's *Diary* for mid-March: 'This morning I received a nice letter from dear Louie Williams, who is barmaid at the Bell Hotel, Gloucester. She enclosed a piece of poetry entitled "Clyro Water" and signed Eos Gwynddwr which she had cut out of last week's *Hereford Times*, not knowing the verses were mine . . .'

Poor Kilvert; when he asked his father, should he publish his poems, the answer was a definite no. What old Mr Kilvert would have made of the great diary, the Lord only knows. The Welsh border, to which, one way or another, I seem to become more and more attached, is haunted by the robust and yet short-lived Francis Kilvert. How hard he worked! How far he walked! How self-revealing he was.

When he walked to Credenhill on a 'lovely and cloudless' March day in 1879, he would not have known of the existence of Thomas Traherne. This amazes me – that the wonderful prose-poet who died in 1674 should not have been read until my lifetime.

James goes to Church

IT IS easy to miss it all, the outside. If it is too wet, you will miss the sharp March rain on your skin. If it is too blowy, you will miss the March birds riding the thermals. How many springs do you think you have, anyway? They say, 'Count your blessings,'but count your springtimes.

Yesterday, it was impossible to count the starlings in their winging murmuration as they flew and folded above the kale field. Several thousand would be a good guess. Had I not gone out in the rain to fetch the milk, I would not have seen them. Or watched the wild clouds looking at themselves in the puddles. Or noted that the wild daffodils, the ones that Dorothy Wordsworth saw and her brother described, were in a yellow ring around the pear tree.

Of course, I got wet and muddy, but 'better'. Not that I was ill or malcontented or anything like that, but I was 'more' than I was before I left the house. After the starlings had gone, a lark sang in their space. The rain filtered through the flints towards the river. Everything was as it usually is in March. Or in *Benedicite*.

I am writing a book about my early days on the Suffolk coast, and dreaded opening the old letters. I thought they would be unendurably sad, or, at least, embarrassing. But quite otherwise. Strong opinions, best love. They are so interesting that I forget to write, and turn their flimsy pages like some captivating novel. Can the recipient be me? There is much untaken advice, lots of gossip, many haunting addresses, particularly in Cornwall. Here we are on Bodmin Moor. What views! And not all of them geographical. And all of these aches and pains in the post. No emails, naturally. But, then, there are no emails now. Which reminds me that I have young friends who have never written me a letter, just postcards from New York. 'What about Posterity?' I tell them. What about it, they reply.

One of my correspondents was the poet James Turner, who has a gothic hand. He went to the eight o'clock and to another service, especially in Cornwall, where he liked a damp slate floor under his knees. His car sloshed through the stream-beds that were the lanes in March. His wife stayed at home to cook us big breakfasts after this ordeal. I thought of the wavering candles and the painted barrel roofs. And still do. Rain is wetter in Cornwall.

James Turner would have approved of the Edmund Centre for Arts and Theology which we are launching at St Edmundsbury Cathedral this month, although I doubt if he would have joined it. Too many Christians.

One of his novels was about Edmund's being murdered in Staverton Thicks, that strange forest where ossifying oak and hollies mount each other like decrepit growth in the final spasms of existence – but which never give up. Nothing grows beneath them. But now and then deer run delicately through their exposed roots, never tripping, always beautiful.

St Edmund is the St Sebastian of Suffolk. He would have been about 29 when they slew him against a tree. A thoughtful wolf took charge of his head. James's dust lies on Bodmin Moor. We put it behind a rock so that it wouldn't blow about.

Passiontide

BIG, handsome birds – green woodpeckers, collared doves – bounce around. The wind is sharp, and there is water, water everywhere. It glitters over the pastures, and makes the thinnest of March ice. Passiontide is inescapable. Passiontide, with its painful, yet sumptuous, hymns and sadness.

The old garden buds. Dressed in two jerseys and a gentlemanly cap, I set to. There is much to do: dead sticks to rake up, edging to sharpen the beds, leaves to rot elsewhere. The white cat says: 'More fool you,' and goes back to sleep. At night, in the spring darkness, a climbing rose taps the pane like Catherine. It joins in the Beethoven, and measures out the silences.

Richard Mabey arrives. We are old, old friends, from way back, and can sit without words, if need be. But we talk, of course. He is to give an official lecture at Essex University, after which there will be a banquet, and I shall take in a sea of young faces, and an ocean of hopes. Towards the end, I will once again be witnessing hundreds of beginnings.

Once, taking a seminar, and not knowing how to fill in the time, and in a room filled with a dozen nationalities, I asked my students to read to me in their own languages. A French girl read Baudelaire at breakneck speed, and a Jewish girl read Genesis in Hebrew. A Japanese student read – what? His words were like the tinkling of glass.

I read them a short story. A local boy read some of his first novel. There was no judgement, only a hearing. My main instruction was to slow them down. Slowing down matins and evensong is an art. Creating spaces. Have I fainted, or fallen asleep? But how I love the familiar voices! And where the lectionary passage does not make sense to the reader, I might let them go on. Such is the nerve of a writer.

Passiontide, and we listen to, among so many other things, Hebrews. We do not know who wrote it, or to whom it was addressed. Christ is the 'effulgence of God's glory', and our high priest.

When the youthful John Bunyan went mad, believing that he had committed an unforgivable sin, his sensible wife turned to Hebrews and read to him: 'Remember where you stand, not before the palpable, blazing fire of Sinai, with the darkness, gloom, and whirlwind, the trumpet blast and oracular voice . . . No, you stand before the city of the living God, heavenly Jerusalem . . . the spirits of good men made perfect, and Jesus the mediator of a new covenant, whose sprinkled blood has better things to tell than the blood of Abel.'

It was this passage that freed Bunyan from religious hysteria, and made him a rational Christian teacher, not to mention an enchanting author.

I must call on my snowdrops. I have thousands of

snowdrops, and mere hundreds of daffodils, and it is easy to believe that these March flowers will wait for my delight. But they will not. They will go. Time will take their bloom, if not their roots. Frosts do not touch them, but I feel I must. March will not have been 'lived' if I do not.

The author of Hebrews meditates on gardening, but to no very great extent, although the New English editors place this passage under the heading, 'The shadow and the real'. It is the real that demands my presence today. Raking, tidying – digging, even.

The King's Bones

COLLECTING the post, there they were, where they had been since time immemorial: my wild daffodils under the plum tree – the ones that Dorothy Wordsworth drew her brother's attention to. Although he did not acknowledge this when he wrote, 'And all at once I saw a crowd, a host, of golden daffodils.'

But their immediacy is true enough. One day, there is just fresh spring grass; the next this golden host, nodding and waving in a chilly breeze. And loud birdsong above them. And the white cat padding through them. And the horses looking through the hazels at them. And then *Narcissus pseudonarcissus*. It descends from the medieval Latin *affodile*, our Lent Lily. How long have they been here, this Wordsworthian patch that spreads? A cold coming they had of it.

Passion Sunday. I take matins. 'Were you there when the sun refused to shine? Oh, sometimes it causes me to tremble, tremble . . .' And, in this instance, passing from the mental sufferings of Jesus as he went the way of the cross. You did not have to walk very far from Jerusalem, or from any Roman city, to see the crucified. It was: 'Keep the peace, or this is what will happen to you.' I often think of this when we give each other the Peace in church. 'The peace of God, David, Meriel, Mrs ... I've forgotten your name.'

Passion Sunday first appeared in the Book of Common Prayer in 1928, so what shall we sing? The sumptuously sad 'O sacred head'; the unsparingly painful 'When I survey'; 'My song is love unknown', which a neighbouring priest wrote for the men in his parish. All of them, and a bitter anthem, and that last glimpse of Jerusalem before the sight faded from those dying eyes. No cheerful goodbyes at the church door.

Floods of crocuses. Scaffolding round the tower. Then carloads of flowers for Easter Day waiting to take over. Early in the week, lunch with a young prison chaplain, myself wondering – marvelling, indeed – at his quiet ability. 'But then I couldn't do what you do,' he says, simply, and I think of the multiplicity of the Church.

Now that King Richard's bones have been translated from a car park to Leicester Cathedral, the author of *Don Quixote*, the first novel, is to be suitably laid to rest. Miguel de Cervantes was almost contemporary with Shakespeare. Don Quixote de Mancha sends up the knightly quest, and is the originator of many of our popular sayings. The following were all said in Spanish before we borrowed them: 'Time out of mind', 'A finger in every pie', 'Put you in a pickle', 'Thank you for nothing', 'No better than she should be', 'Within a stone's throw of it', 'Give the devil his due', 'You've seen nothing yet', 'I begin to smell a rat', 'My memory is so bad that I sometimes forget my own name.'

But there are sayings of his that deserve a new currency: 'Youngsters read it, grown men understand it, and old men applaud it.' Which sent me to the bookshelf to heave down my own, two-volume copy, in French, with wonderful drawings, sometimes two to a page, dated 1836. My name is scribbled in it.

One of Cervantes's sayings is: 'Can we ever have too much of a good thing?' Enthralled, it is well past midnight when I put the Don to bed. 'Mum's the word.'

In the morning, I hurry breakfast to see the eclipse, but invisibility reigns. 'As well look for a needle in a bottle of hay' (Cervantes).

George is Transferred

EASTER WEEK. The lectionary says that George is transferred to the 28th. I transfer the tallest branches of my bamboo to a dark, empty bed to make a wigwam for the sweet peas. The birds sing their heads off, and ponies fly about the hill meadow opposite with streaming tails. It is mild and damp, with bursts of sunshine. Perfect growing weather.

Needing to think of happiness, I think of Thomas Traherne. I find his *Centuries*, the copy that once belonged to my first poet-friend, James Turner. There is a snapshot inside of him reading it. He has come out of hospital, and is in a deckchair, the green volume in his hands. I find the page.

> When I came into the country, and being seated among silent trees and woods and hills, had all my time in mine own hands, I resolved to spend it all, whatever it cost me, in the search of Happiness, and to satiate the burning thirst which Nature had enkindled in me from my youth.
>
> In which I was so resolute that I chose rather to live upon ten pounds a year, and to go in leather clothes and to feed upon bread and water, so that I might have all my time clearly to myself... So that through His blessing I live a free and a kingly life, as if the world were turned again into Eden ...

I am in gardening clothes which are too dreadful to describe here, but Bottengoms Farm is certainly Eden, and loud with birdsong. I sow the sweet-pea seeds, and draw a rake over them. Then it rains like an Amen. Then a second wigwam for the runner beans. Then idling walkers and ecstatic dogs. Then the white cat up an ash tree. Then indoors for some music. Then more Traherne – this time, his appreciation of nature.

> Sublime and perfect: it includes all Humanity and Divinity together. God, Angels, Men, Affections, Habits, Actions, Virtues . . . corporeal things, as Heaven, Earth, Air, Water, Fire, the Sun and Stars, Trees, Herbs, Flowers, Influences . . . the natures of His territories, works, and . . . clearing and preparing the eye of the enjoyer.

I have always loved that 'clearing and preparing the eye of the enjoyer'. Then everything rushes ahead to Mark the Evangelist. Including, of course, the weeds. Never such sumptuous buttercups, such yellowing of the meadows. Such golden (rape) fields. The neighbours' bees arrive. Tom flies overhead, his little plane banking, vanishing, pleased to have an outing.

Then one of those village funerals in which the dead neighbour should have been at the party with us. We talk and drink by the river. It goes its way under the budding willows. Swans pass in majesty. A photograph album is passed round, and there is our missing friend, talking in a garden like this, casting shadows, grinning, staring back at us with the eye of the enjoyer. The bell that tolled for him did so with a small thud, its clapper in a leather bag.

I read St Paul's statement on love, the one that meant everything to Traherne. The poet Anne Ridler called it a masterpiece written by a master of the Affirmative Way. It came to light many years after it was written, on a . . . bonfire! He addressed it to a neighbour called Susanna Hopton. Like bulbs

41

and seeds, it was destined to lie in the darkness before it could flower.

Traherne said: 'We never enjoy ourselves but when we are the joy of others . . . Thus we see the seeds of Eternity sparkling in our natures.' Susanna said that he was a man of cheerful and spritely temper.

He died by the Thames, aged 37, an appreciator of the earth.

APRIL

Julian's Gardener-Christ

CHILLY spring rains, pear blossom clotted on the bough, damp cat, seeds to sow, and a new name to paint on the incumbents board. The reassuring prayer of a mower that starts at first pull. And Easter everywhere. So why not preach on immortality? But first of all, I must get those boyhood visions of graves' balancing rather grim porcelain blooms and hands in glass cases out of my head. 'Immortelles', they call them. Rained on, spotted, rusted, they did a turn.

The Quaker hymn 'Immortal love, forever full, Forever flowing free' does more than this because 'Faith has still its Olivet, And love its Galilee.' Thus we re-map our village. Drenched sticky buds are about to burst. Sheep complain or rejoice – it's hard to know which – in sodden grass.

Taking a country funeral on a wet spring morning is a contradiction in terms. The high language of heaven rules out low thoughts. At the Easter sepulchre, itself a dusty answer, the message is: 'He is not here. He is risen.' Just a heap of linen. And lavish piles of linen here, white as snow. And an angel whose face was like lightning.

And then – maybe because Adrian is getting rid of the last signs of winter outside – this changing of the familiar figure of Jesus, the rabbi-healer, into a gardener, unrecognizable to those who knew him best.

The gardener-Christ entranced Julian of Norwich. She

43

came upon him as he was receiving orders from his master, and dressed roughly in a 'single white coat, old and worn, stained with sweat, tight and short . . . threadbare . . . ready to fall apart at any moment'.

> Outwardly, he looked as if he had been working hard for a long time, but to my inner understanding he seemed to be a beginner, a servant who had never been sent out before. Then I understood: he was to do work that was the hardest and most exhausting possible. He was to be a gardener, digging and banking, toiling and sweating, turning and trenching the ground, watering the plants the while.
>
> And by keeping at this work he would make sweet streams to flow, fine abundant fruits to grow; he would bring them to his lord, and serve them to his taste . . . I thought that in the Lord there was everlasting life and every goodness, except the treasure that was in the earth. And that treasure, too, had its being in the wonderful depth of his eternal love.

Julian's thoughts on the cultural divinity don't come amiss when I watch gardening TV, but it is strangely upsetting that Christ's terrible death was begun in a garden – maybe one in which he had enjoyed watching gardeners at work. Gethsemane.

It was there that he became 'sorrowful and very heavy'. And it was in the garden that he asked his Father to let this cup pass from him – this appalling fate. It was springtime, and new life was everywhere. He, too, was youthful. Passion – interior suffering. The intensity of the hymns.

Samuel Crossman wrote his 'Love unknown' – he had been reading George Herbert – over the hill near here. Tragic language meets in time and place, and above stripped altars. But the spring birds do not speak it. They are noisy with nests and partnerships, and pure life. And the horses on the hill do brief, cumbrous gallops, disappearing and reappearing over the horizon. And this for no apparent reason.

My Little Owls

CERTAIN happiness. Pear blossom. Six a.m. tea. Matins for a dozen in the chancel. Making my sweet-pea wigwam. Seeing strangers pass. Listening to the director of the British Museum on the radio. Watching the manes of the horses on the hill being caught in the wind. Reading Psalm 96.

Eating a miser's meal – pot d'jour, a curling crust, cheese ends, and a wizened apple. Loving my little cat. Not going to the party. Sploshing up the farm track. Remembering the Garretts in Cambridge. Listening to David Holt reading George Herbert. Seeing the boundary ditch full of water. A whisky at bedtime.

Silence. Oaks before ash promising a splash. Re-reading *Swann's Way*. Finding the nail scissors. Visiting the new bookshop in Stoke-by-Nayland. Watching the world greening. Remembering the Turners in Cornwall. Finishing a chapter. Choosing a page of Kilvert's Diary for a sermon. Hearing a climbing rose scratch against the window, like Catherine Earnshaw's escape-me-never hands.

Eating olives. The lawnmower starting at first pull. Feeding chaffinches. Watching Dan draw. The unbelievable scent of bluebells. The kindness of strangers at the hospital. Ash log fires. New jerseys. Giving Vicky plants. Hearing bumble bees. Knowing that the summer spreads before me. Finding true sadness at the passing of Gerald, the village-shop dog.

Finding stitchwort and wild garlic in their accustomed spots. Touching the sun-warmed Roman bricks of the Saxon tower in Colchester and imagining the hands that formed them. Seeing beautiful girls lean on the thousand-year-old doorway. Myself seeing for the thousandth time the house of

John Wilbye, the madrigalist, whose patron gave him a sheep farm for his services. Listening hard, what bliss to hear him singing among the shoppers.

Catching sight of my little owls in the blackthorn, where they have always been. The satisfaction when flowers and creatures know their places. Choosing hymns for Sunday – carefully, of course, as our three churches have three different books. Three parish magazines as well. Three of everything. One of the vicar; one of myself. I consider our oneness.

Rape will soon yellow everything. Its seeds will go to the crusher, and their oil to Waitrose. News from a foreign country comes. Owen has died in Wales. I hear his piano thundering Bach in his cold house. Also our talk as we climb the Black Mountain. How quiet it will be now. No loud voice, no confident keys. He was staunchly Chapel, and went on taking services until his congregation went to God before him. Then he followed. I took him to Shingle Street when he came to stay in Suffolk – as a treat. Was I having a joke? He had shown me mountains, wonders . . . His bewilderment at this time-distance makes me joyful. It was quite something to disconcert Owen.

The April happiness of finding so much promising. To have it all before one. Though not to count the days, but to let them bud and open; the weather to try everything on from gale to serenity; the pages of the current book to fall into chapters; the man from the British Museum to show Shakespeare in a handful of artefacts; and George Herbert to show us the Church as only he can.

The Martyrs

I HAVE been re-reading, as I sometimes do at this time of the year, Willa Cather's novel *Death Comes for the Archbishop*. It tells of an elegant French priest sent to carve out a diocese in

New Mexico in the 1850s, when, by nature, he would have much preferred to read Madame de Sévigné in the gardens of Italy.

Although an aesthete, however, Fr Jean Marie Latour possesses a spiritual toughness that makes him the right choice for this enormous work. Thus, in unforgettable prose, he rides off.

New Mexico was converted ages before by the Jesuits, but the faith has been distorted by folk-art, etc., and Latour's task is really more difficult than if he had to bring the Church to where there was no Christianity at all. Cather's writing is that of a great traveller, and her psychology that of a supreme artist of the 1920s. Her young priest, who is often dreaming of Paris and thinking in poetry, does all that is demanded of him, and dies an old archbishop.

Latour comes to mind in April because it is when we should remember Alphege, Archbishop of Canterbury, who was murdered in 1012 by some drunks who had kidnapped him. Like Becket – and like a surprising number of priests who hoped to evade high office in order to live as their personalities required them to live – he had been forced to leave his cell in the ruins of Bath to be Bishop of Winchester. He was thirty. Twenty years later, he was a reluctant Archbishop of Canterbury.

The convention of Danegeld was in full swing when the northern raiders demanded ransoms to stop their burnings and rapes. In 1012, they demanded the enormous ransom of £48,000. The King was too scared to do anything; so it was Archbishop Alphege who held a council, at which, instead of talking about money, he reminded everyone of the laws of Christian civilization, and how these must prevail at all costs in the face of lawlessness and inhumanity.

Alphege's position and courage were very like those of so many martyrs, including Becket – and Dietrich Bonhoeffer, hanged by the Gestapo at Flossenbürg in 1945, the pattern never changing over a thousand years. The mockery and violence was that of the soldiery before the crucifixion.

This is what Bonhoeffer wrote on the eve of his execution. He had been in New York – he need not have returned to the Nazis:

> O God, early in the morning I cry to you.
> Help me to pray
> And to concentrate my thoughts on you:
> I cannot do this alone.
> In me there is darkness,
> But with you there is light;
> I am lonely, but you do not leave me;
> ... In me there is bitterness, but with you there is patience;
> I do not understand your ways,
> But you know the way for me ...
> Restore me to liberty ...
> Lord, whatever this day may bring,
> Your name be praised.

Mark's Parable

AND the rain it raineth every day. The white cat is writing to the RSPCA to complain about my cruelty at allowing this to happen. To have to be dried out on a radiator every morning. It is intolerable. But the horses are animated by the mighty showers, and career over the hill, their happy sloping bodies showering the grass. Sepia skies are streaked with gold. Things are coming up in the beds with all their might. One might be in Wales.

On Sunday, I preached on St Mark, a fast favourite. What style! His Gospel is brief and brilliant. He is the Ezekiel of the New Testament, youthful and charismatic, addressing the universe. His symbol is borrowed from Ezekiel's winged lion, the noise of whose wings was like a great torrent, or cloudburst.

Ezekiel said, having to explain himself, one supposes: 'A spirit lifted me up and carried me along, and I went full of exultation, the hand of the Lord strong upon me.' Mark, too, is a winged intellect who knows how to keep the pages turning. His Gospel contains no nativity, no holy boyhood, but opens with a shout: 'Prepare a way for the Lord!'

It is only in Mark that we have the parable of the sower, and a command to stay awake. He is a broadcaster – a word for throwing seed this way and that in springtime. He knows a lot about waste, hazard, and survival. Its agricultural imagery, for the first time in two thousand years, falls short of familiarity these days.

Who was Mark? As the cousin of Barnabas, he was probably from Cyprus. Paul took him on those long walks into Asia Minor. He and Timothy. Paul is old, battered, and near to death. He tells his young friends that it is their turn to pursue integrity, love, and peace, because: 'I have run the great race, have finished the course, and the prize awaits me.'

My favourite Pauline instruction is when he tells Timothy: 'Pick up Mark, and bring him with you, for I find him a useful assistant . . . When you come, bring the cloak I left with Carpus, and the books; above all, my notebooks.'

Like Mark's Gospel, John Keats's poem 'The Eve of St Mark' is unfinished. Not concluded. But it might have been written at this moment.

> The city streets were clean and fair
> From wholesome drench of April rains;
> And, on the western window panes,
> The chilly sunset faintly told
> Of unmatur'd green vallies cold . . .

49

A girl closes an old book, and walks to evensong in Winchester Cathedral, her head full of puzzling thoughts about its 'legend pages'. Curious and beautiful things sparkle on it, such as:

> Candlesticks John saw in heaven,
> The winged Lion of Saint Mark,
> And the Covenantal Ark
> With its many mysteries,
> Cherubim and golden mice.

St Peter's, Sudbury

WHEN St Peter's, Sudbury, was handed over to the Redundant Churches' Trust, I was so wounded that I felt I could never enter it again. Had the diocese never seen its billowing processions, or its gaslight playing on Bodley's gloriously soaring altarpiece, or heard Mr Vinnicombe raising the roof on the organ, or listened to us all – from the mayor down – in full voice at evensong? Had it never looked up at our canopy of honour? Did not Pevsner say that St Peter's convincingly expressed our wealth?

Was there no one living who could plead its sheer loveliness? Or at least its ability to plant a heart-stopping Anglicanism in the heart of a worshipping child?

Anyway, with an hour before the dentist, I stepped into St Peter's, and into what must be the most enchanting tea-shop in England. The lighting had something to do with it. Bodley sparkled, the slender arcades, cut in 1460, were sharp as knives. Anyone looking around could not fail to see what High Church meant. The mayor arrived in a procession of two, and praised something or somebody. Admittedly, there was no music, but there was a kind of market-day prayer.

I thought how Thomas Gainsborough, born a few yards

away, would have noted a certain perpetuity in the Suffolk face. But what I chiefly saw was a late Gothic interior which was both heavenly and domesticated. And, of course, seated on each corner of the tower were my beloved griffins seeing off the Devil from all directions. They watch like meerkats and are as unredundant as anything can be. Half a millennium of wild weather has failed to bring them down. From the burning of martyrs to myself singing Merberke, the curious antics of the faithful, everything 'religious' has passed before their stony gaze.

And now the scent of tea and cakes, England's own incense, rises from below. Wonderful bells which still ring. And great gold clocks which still sound the hours. And the organ seat on which sat my small brother, Gerald, learning to play.

The spring arrived on Friday. I took the pot plants outside to make the most of it. They flourished immediately. The fine rain was a gift to every leaf. I threw poppy seed around on spare ground and threw nice old bits of this and that to the nesting birds. I wrote a song for a trio and read about poor Archbishop Alphege who, in April 1012, was murdered by hooligans on the Thames. This cruel and inane act would begin an empowering of the Church. Thus April goes its way, warmer now, the bitter wind gone at last.

One thing leads to another. Searching for the right size flowerpots, I turn out things which might come in handy but clearly have not. And 50 jam jars at least on the sagging shelf. Ancient farmhouses are so accommodating, as are vestries. The marvellous black and white photographs of Edwin Smith, taken just after the war, reveal the untidiness of churches at that time, the scattered hymn-books, the bedraggled surplices hanging from pegs, the dipping frontals, even a dead sparrow. A bike against the wall. In summer an ocean of wild flowers drowning the gravestones. Also framed groups, the rector centre and almost smiling faces.

We are very neat and tidy at Wormingford and we use the hearse for our bookstall. Did it long ago bump down to Bottengoms Farm? Its wheels say, 'So many last journeys, such short trips, such sensible iron steering.'

William Morris in Iceland

THERE is quite a lot of noise about silence at the moment. Quietness suits me better. Silence cuts out the wind in the plum trees, Mozart, etc. Is quietness the diminutive of silence? Not to me. It is too great for that. Dean Swift said that the best doctors in the world were Doctor Diet, Doctor Quiet, and Doctor Merryman. Not that I take my quiet medicinally. It lies around me in various states of non-noisiness, which are broken now and then by the white cat falling off a radiator.

I am doing duty in the long walk, a three-hour job once a year, when the winter litter is raked up and the spring grass made ready for the mower. All kinds of destinations lead from it: for my badgers, the way to the boundary stream; for me, the way out. I try not to stick to the narrow way so as to avoid making a bare patch. A couple of cuts and the long walk will deserve being written in capitals. But not yet. Though the grass is green. The badgers snout about in it for worms.

Such winter-spring skies; such rowdy birds travelling across them, blown-about gulls and the like. Such shafts of sunshine. Yet an April quietness prevails. And the clean grass looks hopeful.

Soon, I must come in and correct some proofs. To do this, I must stop reading, and follow the text line by line. This is a nice, mechanical task that takes ages, and that cannot be hurried. And is best done in silence, or at least quietly. The study clock ticks through the sentences and would miss out tea, given a chance.

Now and then I think of popes, archbishops, etc., settling in, hanging up their new clothes, staring at their new names on the envelopes, trying out their new blessings in the mirror. St Jerome said: 'The face is the mirror of the mind, and eyes without speaking confess the secrets of the heart.' He also said, reading Ephesians: 'Never look a gift horse in the mouth.'

So, what must I read, with Easter passed? With my proofs done? With the birds kicking up a row? With the angel announcing Mary's pregnancy? With bluebells budding in Arger Fen? With the long walk looking a treat?

First, I must finish William Morris's *Icelandic Journals*, which are not as cold as they sound. Warm-hearted, in fact. He was 37, and losing his wife to Dante Gabriel Rossetti; so, drawn by the sagas to an unlikely destination, he set sail for – Iceland. And its surprising flowers. Famous as the author of *The Earthly Paradise*, he was received by the Icelanders with honour and love.

The Victorians journeyed to Iceland in order to find a society nobler than their own. Not a paradise, necessarily, but a better place than Dickens's Britain, and its gross materialism. Morris arrived there in July 1871. Now read on. He returned two months later: 'So there I was in London at last, well washed, and finding nobody I cared for dead,' and his head full of flowers, and his pockets full of diary, and his heart full of Socialism – a dear, great, still young man. 'Topsy' to his friends, and an antidote to our current thinking.

MAY

Mrs Eliot

TO LITTLE GIDDING, the three of us.

> You would find the hedges
> White again, in May, with voluptuary sweetness.

And, of course, we did.

Long ago, I attended T. S. Eliot's memorial service in Westminster Abbey, and heard Sir Alec Guinness read this third *Quartet* from the pulpit. It was written during the Blitz, and that fiery turmoil could not have been further away than pensive Huntingdonshire. My aunt Daisy Upjohn lived there. So did red kites.

It remains a county of non-emphatic things, such as the unlisted flower that my botanist friend, Stephen Garrett, found in a dried-up pond. It was a long drive by track and motorway. And there was the dull façade, which I have never found dull at all, and the bumpy evidence of human presence in the grass, and of God's presence everywhere. You can see for miles.

The hospitality of plainness is what is offered – is what the little king was offered. And how strange for him to be in Cromwell-land! Where the entire book of Psalms was recited daily. Now and then, I have sat in the chapel and thought I could still hear the holy drone.

The east window once contained a rarely depicted Joseph

54

of Arimathaea, but now it frames greening trees, which wave against the glass. The seating is collegiate, the east end, font, and commandments are enduring brass. Outside, John Ferrar's tomb tilts. I want to stay for hours, but our hired car must be returned by six, and so we join the workers on their way home, we and the red kites. Pilgrimages are like this. An effort, a prayer, a conclusion.

Back home, the white cat sits where we left her, on the disintegrating brick wall. Ivies and moss hold it together. She always waits until the sun warms it up. She meets us with restrained joy, and a lively appetite; a holy animal. Adrian comes to cut the grass.

I remember having dinner in London with Valerie, Eliot's widow. It has been pouring with rain, and when she takes her coat off she is covered with – sapphires.

'Mrs Eliot!' I say.

'*Cats*, dear,' she explains. A homely Yorkshire woman.

In 'A Dedication to my Wife', Eliot wrote:

To whom I owe the leaping delight
That quickens my senses in our wakingtime.

There are photos of them, not young, not old, smiling into the camera. I never asked if she had been to Little Gidding. I said I knew Yorkshire, a little. An American publisher and his wife were giving us dinner at the Dorchester. It was all so unlikely, yet happening. Like life itself.

I watched the last train to Suffolk make its drenched way. The night was light. Rainwater streamed down the carriage window. Footballers got out here and there. I felt wide awake, too. And now, all these years later, I can't remember what we said or what we ate. Just damp clothes and sapphires in a London hotel, and a generous American publisher helping us on with our coats. 'It was before your time,' I tell the white cat.

Although she is no spring chicken. How beautiful she is, how perfect.

In my T. S. Eliot poems, *Old Possum's Book of Practical Cats* is sandwiched between *Four Quartets* and *Murder in the Cathedral*. I expect he decreed this. The wills of poets are adamant – famously, where Valerie was concerned. Solicitors, too, follow instructions. But writers tend to lose the way, going off at a tangent, chasing hares. Dreaming. Trying to think of what somebody said 40 years ago, and not of sapphires in the rain.

Marigolds

A SUMMER day in April. The windows wide, the robins noisy. A visit to the old horse-pond to see the marsh marigolds in all their glory. Their Latin name comes from *kalathos*, Greek for 'goblet'. Their leaves hide the water, and their petals are cupped above the frog spawn. The artist John Nash adored their annual sowing. 'Never pass up a pond,' he used to tell me.

Mine – one at the top of the garden, and one below – are spring-fed, their surfaces out of sight. The plough horses drank from them before and after work, swigging up such gallons of water that it looked as if they would drink them dry. Now they are wildflower oases from which I rake last summer's leavings.

Pear and apple blossom is on the point of showing, and the vine on the south wall is in bud. Who could stay inside? 'Me,' the white cat, no lover of fresh air, says. 'Give me a nice radiator any day.'

Bloomsbury-set reminiscences on the radio. How sickly they all were. No antibiotics. Nash used to regale me with Garsington antics, and how Lady Ottoline Morrell would often be at her wits' end to keep her 'lions' happy. Once, Nash said, she made them play football in the barn on a wet day,

D. H. Lawrence included, and herself as goalie, and when he was running a cold, sent him home in a huge motor-car, wrapped in her fur coat.

For hostesses, country-house weekends were perilous, with boredom and discomfort nibbling at the edges. The wonderful short-story writer Saki Munro, killed on the Western Front in 1916, made them the venue of his most pitiless tales. And, of course, the home of Tobermory, a gossiping cat.

But my cat has something better to do than to tell tales. Such as to worship the sun, or find a good lap. Idleness to her is a profession, and one has to look one's best to practise it.

This is the moment when the Traherne Association sends me its newsletter. A new window in Hereford Cathedral captures his appreciation of the earth, never more so than at this moment. He could not tell the difference between poetry and prose. He was a young man in a leather suit who thought that the best way to live was to lie under a tree. We – you and I – live in an 'endless sphere' of 'endless pleasures', or we should: otherwise, something is amiss.

When I think of Traherne, I also think of those who continue to celebrate him in his own countryside, Herefordshire, and in his own parish, Credenhill, and with his own 'singer', Richard Birt.

The teachers, saints, and singers of the English Church have a habit of dropping out of sight until a knowing hand recaptures them, and places them where they belong in the lectionary. Never more so than Traherne, that ecstatic voice.

I met him through the poet James Turner, when I was a youth; he died ages ago. His widow said: 'Choose one of his books to remember him.' So I chose his Traherne: *Poems, Centuries and Three Thanksgivings*, edited by Anne Ridler. 'A stranger here Strange Things doth meet, Strange Glories see.'

The Padstow 'Oss

THE white cat is given to loftiness in her advancing years, sitting high up in fruit trees, and on the ledge of a Tudor chimney, purring away, looking down on us, bursting with achievement. As is the late and lovely spring. Never such a rush of flowers, such drugging scents. Put work aside. Simply be. For – who knows? – such days might not come my way again. The horses roll on their backs; the trees grow greener by the minute. Best of all, both white and purple fritillaries have multiplied in the orchard grass.

It is May Day, the day of days – the day that we once spent in Padstow, drinking beer at 8.30 in the morning as the 'Obby 'Oss [hobby horse] was led out to a haunting song, to process through the slate streets – perhaps the most moving folk festival in Britain. Quite why it should be so escapes all explanation. You have to dance in its wake to prove it so.

And then, those with whom we danced are no longer with us to provide evidence. They have drunk and sung and leapt their way ahead and out of sight, leaving a little music behind – and a pile of curling photos.

My old friend Michael Mayne – for a memorable decade, Dean of Westminster – placed much of his Christian philosophy in an enchanting book, *Learning to Dance*.

> In many ways, I am an unlikely dancer, having only fully mastered the waltz and the Dashing White Sergeant, and, at the age of ten, a passable sailors' hornpipe, yet the ideas of the invitation to the cosmic dance, and of dance as a metaphor for our assorted lives in this mysterious, dancing universe, have gone on expanding in my mind . . .

Jesus despaired of 'this generation', of its joylessness and ingratitude. 'You are like children calling out to other children, We have piped for you and you did not dance.'

Some years ago, two young neighbours of mine danced down the aisle of Blythburgh Church, in Suffolk, after their wedding. If one is going to dance in church, it may as well be in this angelic building. David, of course, danced before the Ark of the Covenant, being a great poet. In one of his psalms, he turns mourning into dancing, and they conclude with the fortissimo dance music and words of the four final psalms.

Mayne might be said to have taught cosmic dancing wherever he went, and finally at Salisbury, where I 'met' George Herbert when I was in my 20s.

The sun is hot on the study window, the May wind chilly. My old friend Antony Pritchett, Vicar of Pickering, is about to pay his annual visit, and we shall do a bit of exploring and a great deal of talking. Each year, I have to provide somewhere different to go, but the talking takes off in fresh directions without the least trouble.

'When did you first decide to be a priest?'

'When I was six.'

When did I first decide to be a writer? Who can tell? 'How is Merbecke?' Merbecke is Antony's dog.

Friends in Yorkshire or Cornwall, or in a Barbara Pym novel, or wildly dancing in scripture, or at this moment giving the churchyard grass its first good back and sides, are given movement by May time. I am, too; and the mower is raring to go at the first pull. The poppy seed I scattered is up; the climbers I tied back are in bud. So soon. So on the go, everything. 'Allus on the goo,' the neighbours used to say – and not approvingly.

In North Carolina

IT IS one of those grey mornings – the west wind soft and contemplative, the animals munching the May grass, nose to nose.

The radio goes in one ear and out the other until, suddenly, I am all attention. A name is mentioned, then a moral position. It is Obama. For no accountable reason, it suggests to me another name: James Baldwin.

He and I have been sent for a walk in London by his publisher, Michael Joseph. What is more, we have been given £10 for lunch. I am to persuade him to cut some pages from his latest novel; it is not at all unusual for a writer to go off at a tangent in a story, and start another story. This is what James has done.

James is a New York novelist who is deservedly at the height of his fame; a slight, nervous man in his thirties, who, unlike most of us, is all physicality, clutching my hand as we stroll along, and nervous, like a kitten. I am awed by his genius, and ready to accept his fury when I mention these errant pages. But he says: 'Of course, of course.'

I tell him how much I loved his previous novel, *Giovanni's Room*. We are at peace. We have been sent out like children with the publisher's pocket money. So what shall we do, where shall we go? London roars around us. I know it a little, and James not at all. We keep to the streets. No St Paul's, no museums. No Obama in the White House; and, so far as I'm concerned, no comprehension of racism.

The radio is talking about Alistair Cooke and the American Civil War. My only experience of its unresolved tragedy was when I stayed in one of those *Gone With the Wind* mansions in South Carolina, and found a grave in the garden. Surrounded by mournful yews, it was that of a 24-year-old Lieutenant. It had been dug in the garden in which he had played as a boy.

The first night I was there, the owners, who were in New York, telephoned to say, 'Close all the shutters – there's going to be a gale.' And there certainly was. The trees in the park bowed to the ground, and the big timber-framed house trembled – rather like James on our London stroll.

It was all unlike Suffolk, where the flint church-towers and the trees withstood the storms and the occasionally swollen rivers. It is what the British notice abroad, the way the rain falls and the winds blow.

Walking near Sydney with my brother, he laughed when I treated the spitting rain as I would have done a brief shower at home, but in seconds we were soaked to the skin. Ditto the New South Wales sun, which looked merely pleasant from the veranda, but cooked one alive on the lawn.

I preach on the sayings of Jesus: how his hearers did not take notes, but, although he frequently spoke to congregations like a rabbi, there is no record of anyone in the New Testament recording what he said. Yet his teachings are a bit like those of a single author, both in style and message. Long after the message, long after the crucifixion, those who heard him speak would have told their children, and those they met, what he had said – and maybe how he said it.

He was a great poet. He was furious with those who spoke and did not act, possibly thinking of those of his own race, who sang the Psalms, which was the Jews' hymn-book, beautifully, but failed to live by the words. Christianity is but music for many people.

A Fluid Landscape

'WE WILL have breakfast with the nightingales,' Romane announced. So off we drove through the waking town. Except for us, everyone was going to school or to work. The suburbs ended abruptly; then came a kind of overture to the marshes and rivulets, with tall, greening trees, after which appeared a far distant coast that the sea had torn to ribbons over the years.

We set up our meal on a little gorse plateau, and already the nightingales were at their chook-chook-chooking and piu-piu-piuing, though unseen. The coffee and rolls had stayed hot, and a white and blue tablecloth had been laid. The gorse was in bloom with a vengeance. When Carolus Linnaeus first witnessed flowering gorse, they said, he burst into tears, overwhelmed by its glory.

Far ahead, dominating the watery land was the tower of All Saints', Brightlingsea. It stared down on Alresford Creek and across to us, making itself felt as became the church of a Cinque Port, and a solid thing in a fluid landscape. We talked in a desultory fashion about what should, or could, or must not happen to our living back home, and seemingly in another country.

More and more nightingales sang; more and more marshes glittered. The sun stoked itself up. We sampled Marit's marmalade, and felt irresponsible. Now and then, seagulls were blown about over our heads.

I found myself remembering a figure from these parts, the Revd Gerald Montague Benton, an archaeologist, one of those learned men who blinked through their glasses and whose apparent easiness and civility concealed an iron will where faculties were concerned. What brought him to these salt marshes, to this liquid meeting of earth and sky? Amazingly, his parish church had been shaken to bits by an earthquake in 1884. But the instability of things remained apparent. Also the brightness of things.

Sprawling above the crashing Atlantic Ocean in Cornwall, I saw no point in ever doing anything again. Be a layabout – cease. Listen. But then we must get home for lunch. The white cat, who is sloth incarnate, will be lying on her warm brick wall, starving to death.

And I must take a hundredth look at my white and purple fritillaries. Never so many. They are blooming in the orchard, and on old grass paths, along with countless other wildflowers. The long cold winter held them back, then the spring said:

'Now!' And thus this racing flood of blooms. The ancient ash tree is suddenly young again, every twig ending with fat buds, and the mower goes at first pull.

We all sit in the chancel at matins. The cold interior has preserved the prolific Easter flowers and distilled their scent. The Epistle is St James's reminder: 'Every good gift, and every perfect gift is from above, and cometh down from the Father of lights, with whom there is no variableness, neither shadow of turning.' What language!

What is actually coming down at this moment is the first spring rain. It drenches the lambs in the far field, the joyful dogs, the conversing horses. It ruffles the surface of the ponds, and polishes up the view. St James speaks of self-deception, of our being hearers and not doers of the Word. He is so beautiful in his reproaches. Who could not take him to heart?

Return of Aldeburgh

IT HAS been one of those bursting-with-life May weeks, thus the apologetic smiles of the old friends in the obituary column of the newspaper. 'We didn't mean to go in May!' A memorial service will be announced later. I see their houses, hear their voices. It will need practice to live without them. But May, when there is so much to do! The white cat has no patience with death. She chooses a warm brick wall to purr on. Nine lives, of course. But she can't count. Neither can I, for that matter. So I do my accounts for the accountant, small sums from great matters. I listen to Fauré and Britten.

The cousins from Kent turn up – 'No, we have never been to Aldeburgh.' So off we set to the Suffolk coast, where the temperature drops. I show them Benjamin Britten's grave. Imogen Holst's, too. There they lie in the vast churchyard, one behind the other. But these deaths are mine, and cannot be shared.

The sea glitters. It has a gravelly voice. It rakes the pebble beach. Victorian ladies, bent double, searched it for amber on Sunday afternoons. Amber comes from the Arabic for a yellowish resin that is derived from extinct conifers. Sometimes, an insect has been trapped in it, like a jewel that once ran and breathed. Amber comes from ambergris. Aldeburgh women wore hefty necklaces of this fossil. But, to me, every stone on the beach was precious – told a tale.

The North Sea rocked its flint shore about restlessly all day, all night. Yet it was full of plants. Their roots went deep, and were beyond disturbance. We went to the bookshop, of course. Aldeburgh has a great bookshop, and a great fish and chip shop. What more could one ask for? But, like this week's papers, it is full of the names of the departed. Walking in the churchyard is like being at a party where one needs no introduction.

The wide church is bright with polished brass and flowers. I visit the bust of the realist poet George Crabbe, and the window to Britten by John Piper, and everywhere there are memorials to my friends the Garretts.

It is an uncloudy place with everything hard and bright. All the drowned fishermen have been immortalized by oceanic movement. This is where I was taught botany, and how to walk against the wind. It was Bank Holiday, but not festive. A mild gale polished us up. In the Moot Hall I gazed on the mayoral portraits, and imagined Peter Grimes's trial – his sentence to be the borough's scapegoat on the marshes. One brave young man dived into the sea and made a splash.

Back in Wormingford, I take matins, and learn that only God can order the unruly wills and affections of sinful men, although I must love what he commands, and desire what he promises. Faith often asks this. That we should want what God offers. And then comes St James's unforgettable reminder: 'Every good gift, and every perfect gift cometh down from the

Father of lights, with whom there is no variableness, neither shadow of turning.' Constancy. That is the thing.

In Aldeburgh Church, I sat briefly where I sat when I was young. Rehearsals rather than the finished music filled my head, perfection not being achieved until endless practice. Britten, tireless, edgy. The ghosts of great gales and hardships. And always the marine light, the aerial version of endlessly polished flints, and a gift worth having.

No Water Rates

'TWO can play at that game,' I tell the white cat. Perfectly still, and in perfect profile, she is observing existence. Not so the young blackbird trapped between my palms as I prevent it from braining itself against the pane. Pure terror must be its brief lot.

Stillness is much advocated in Christianity, although one would never guess it. As the years pile up, one tends to withdraw from parish 'liveliness', and, whether one wants it or not, into a degree of contemplation. 'Ye watchers and ye holy ones.' Thomas Hardy's favourite scripture, and a favourite of mine, is 1 Kings 19, when God is not in wind or earthquake or fire, but is 'a still small voice'. The quotation is on the memorial window in Stinsford Church.

I suspect that this is how most of us hear God; although George Herbert listened to Christ conversationally. The temple boy heard God telling him what to do via a priest, and a discredited one at that. In our day, more and more of us listen to him talking via nature. I hear him in poetry, philosophy, and natural noise, harmonic or otherwise. Although, like cheerfulness, scripture will keep breaking in.

The old friend from Athens is here. Like me, she is a chronic reader. There was an American literary critic who confessed: 'They tell me that life is the thing, but I prefer reading.'

'One more chapter, or one more page,' I would beg at bedtime. I know people who prefer reading to eating. They look quite good on it. I frequently find the Lessons too abridged, not to say cut to the bone, and do not always obey the lectionary. Also, I love the varied voices. Long ago, an old farmworker was so transported with what he found on the lectern that he would look up to declare in his rich Suffolk voice: 'That was very fine – I'll read that again.' And he did.

The old churches are full of recitations, full of tales that had to come to an end. They were our portion. Lodged in our head, they tend to float about, although often there is no escape. God's still small voice is never raised – although, heaven knows, it should be, sometimes.

My water supply must be cleansed, tested, drained. Many of us are not on the mains, but on a medieval system. The water table of the Stour allows us a bath and a cup of tea if we ask politely. No rates, of course, just free flow. I dress for this ancient gift. I visit the springs in the wilds, then rake the ditch. Then I clamber into a kind of mud chamber to bale out its silky contents. So far, a bishop hasn't called.

This task is followed by various grand neighbours, none of whom descends into the black depths, owing to their possessing a ram. I'll go no further. Sufficient to add that if you have not progressed from turning on the cold tap, our advanced hydraulics will be beyond your grasp.

Not that I envy you. Clothed annually in pure mud, then in sparkling stream water, such as Chaucer or the Wife of Bath might have used, who could envy what falls from a shower? Mudlarks are at a premium these days. Mind you, it puts one's fingernails into mourning. And one is apt to carry a rivery smell for a day or two, which makes the clean cat look up.

The Cornish Funeral

AS I SORT papers for the British Library, a toppling pile of letters from Cornwall says something like: 'We dare you to read us; for here is your early self.' They are from the poet and novelist James Turner, my first writer-friend, mentor, and, I suppose, hero. He looked unheroic in his indeterminate tweeds, and with his bonfire of a pipe.

He and his wife, Cathy, had moved from Suffolk to Cornwall in the 1950s, thus this huge correspondence. He wrote in a gothic hand or on a gothic typewriter. Publishers fell before him. Critics were consigned to hell. My own work was put through the mill. But he never lost his power over us, the youthful group of artists and writers he had left behind in East Anglia; and, once a year, whether at Christmas or in summer, I would take the blissful Penzance train to stay with him in a series of stone houses near the Atlantic Ocean.

So I began to re-read the answers to my letters. They ended abruptly in May 1975, when I once again travelled west, but to a funeral. Alone but for the youthful rector, I took James to Truro to be cremated. I read his poems in St Teath's. All the way – about 30 miles, and in an early heatwave – I saw signposts pointing to our walks, the Cheesewring, St Juliot – where Thomas Hardy courted his wife, and where, bewilderingly, after her death (for their marriage sounds to us anything but happy), he set some of the greatest love poems in the language – to slate-floored pubs, where we talked books by the hour and he urged me to leave 'cold old East Anglia and to come west'.

Thus the day passed with little getting done. I had forgotten how cross he could get. People who had long dropped out of sight re-entered the present. So busy were we with them that it is a wonder either of us got anything done. James broadcast from Plymouth on gardening. He wrote self-confessed thrillers to finance his poetry; he made the usual freelance living.

In my early 20s, he and I read Herbert in Suffolk churches. His voice was perfect for this. And my favourite photo of him is where he sits in a deckchair, holding the works of Thomas Traherne. 'Take something from the library to remember him,' Cathy said. So I took this.

His Anglicanism was 1920s Lancing Chapel, plus Herbert and Traherne, plus a certain chilliness. We always seemed to kneel in the dampest corner of a church for the eight o'clock communion, which in Cornwall was frigid. He needed to get away before 'all them' – the 11 o'clock congregation – appeared.

He had tuberculosis, which his wife called bronchitis just to soften it a bit. He thought that tobacco did it good. He typed away in what I thought in those days was a nice smelly fog. They were psychics, and when they moved house they needed or looked for a good haunting as the rest of us required good plumbing.

Two close friends could not have been less alike. Yet this letter-hoard is proof of our devotion. His wild romanticism also required that I placed his ashes beneath a rock on Bodmin Moor.

'Don't throw them into the wind,' they advised, 'or you will find some of them in your turn-ups.'

My Birthplace, Acton, Suffolk

'HERE is the church' – a fat gooseberry; 'here is the steeple' – the tuft; and 'here come all the country people' – the juicy pips. It was always St Peter's, Sudbury, Suffolk, when I said this.

Yesterday, I walked in the small town, remembering this and that. Here is the north door, thinned to a biscuit by the centuries. Here, on its left side, is the stoup – dry now, but medieval fingers once touched holy water in it. Here are a few church-hugging tombs, even if most of the

Sudbury congregations are being run over regularly by buses.

It is a cold May morning, and the familiar borough could well have been Proust's Combray, somewhere where memory is put to work.

Quite a few people are sitting about – sitting, at ten in the morning! It would never have happened in my day. They cannot all have had a funny turn. Nice railings, to which Canon Hughes never chained his black bike. Gorgeous reredos, under a dust sheet. Wonderful bells, which Father listened to, standing out in the garden on practice night.

A writer's task is to make ordinariness extraordinary. This is not something that a writer can help doing. 'That boy's head!' they said. Whatever next!

I was looking for half a dozen butter-knives with bone handles. 'Bone handles, you say, sir? Try the charity shops.' Lots of these. Fat ladies, scrawny old chaps. The jewellers' where Father bought Mother's rings.

Andrew has loaned me a book that I have been searching for all my life, *The Claimants to the Estates of William Jennens late of Acton, near Long Melford, Suffolk.* Andrew and I were born in this village. Mr Jennens had been its squire, a bachelor who drowned in money. Birmingham iron channelled rivers of it to his Suffolk address. He filled vases with it, put it under the bed and in the cellars, gave it to anyone who would be good enough to take it, but still it flooded in his direction. A will was no use; it washed away wills. He went to church on Sundays, and sat below his marble father, and I hope some of his money came the Revd Mr Bickersteth's way. When, at last, Mr Jennens died, the litigants swarmed in. But the lawyers were too smart for them, and, during the next 40 years, took it all. The Jennens case entertained society and enthralled Charles Dickens, who put it to use in *Bleak House*.

I was less interested in this scandal, however, than in the author's description of Acton Church, where both Andrew and

I were baptized, and where my father's name is on the Great War memorial. Not that anything happened to him: just there and back to the Dardanelles, the usual thing. Before this mishap, he sang in the choir.

The 1877 book never mentions Perp. and Dec. or the mighty de Bures brass – the finest, some say, in England. But it adores the varnished seating and the floor space, and that 'in the north-west corner of the churchyard a place of accommodation had been erected for those who during divine service may have to satisfy the calls of nature'.

The north-west corner is where my ancestors lie. It is now the wild plot. Our crosses will be floating in cow-parsley, one of the loveliest sights in England. But poor old Mr Jennens, drowning in Birmingham money and being dubbed a miser, which he never was. Just a lonely man who could not swim in it. Thirty or so years after his burial, they pulled his mansion down, brick by brick, and sold each one.

The Comforter

MAY – and all of summer ahead. Cool Pentecostal winds are tossing the lilacs. Jean's horses shelter behind what will soon be a white wall of blossom. I eat my breakfast to the stern words of the Chief Rabbi as he preaches on the Fourth Commandment. The white cat descends from on high to plead starvation, her current roost being the top of a cupboard in the old dairy. And so the day begins – most days, to be truthful.

Writers call to tell me about their books in progress. Hearing their names on the radio, F. Scott Fitzgerald and his wife, Zelda, I take down *The Great Gatsby* and *Tender is the Night*. They are dusty, yellowing. But not when I turn the page. Wildly attractive young men are on the make; disastrously lovely girls are getting hurt. But the prose – so timeless!

It is just after breakfast, however, when novels must be kept in their place on the shelf. The visiting novelists are professionally silent on their work, for there is little more tedious than having to hear a tale half-told. We have lamb chops and new potatoes for lunch, and talk about how some authors remain, while others, for no apparent reason, have their day, and then go away. Or, rather, line up in alphabetical order in the library, not even pleading 'Read me!' Read once, they have more to say, but no one is listening.

I preach on the Comforter – what a marvellously inspired name for the Holy Spirit. The Comforter. When you think of it, the Lord's friends had such a brief apprenticeship for what they had to do – a little less than three years, and that on the hoof. And the crowds! 'What was that he said?' They were fearful, filled with inadequacy, watched by the police.

When I read the Acts of the Apostles (what a good title), or the history of the beginning of the Church, I am as much moved by the plight of these men as by their genius. They are so like us, and yet so unlike us, being the commissioned spreaders of the teachings of Jesus.

At first, their dependency on him made them vulnerable to a fright verging on terror. While he was with them, they could be immature, even silly: in what order should they sit at heaven's high table? And now they remembered thinking, 'What will happen to us after he has "gone" – when we are on our own?'

Mercifully, there were the old feasts, particularly Pentecost, to hold life together, to keep its shape. This is what festivals are for. Then came the odd number – 11. Eleven would never do. They had to be the perfect Twelve. So they drew straws and the lot fell on Matthias. It did not matter if posterity knew no more of him than his name. He was 12th man.

This done, reports Luke, who was an excellent writer, and usually careful with facts, the house in which they gathered

71

shook. And there was the sound of a mighty rushing wind. And they were able to communicate, to anyone who listened, what they had heard.

A flaming intelligence and holiness rose from their heads, which would be commemorated in the mitre, and Peter would preach the very first sermon. His text was taken from Joel. And the Comforter came to all of us. 'Breathe on me, breath of God,' we sang, some 20 of us.

JUNE

Laurie Lee

PENTECOST – 70 days after the resurrection, when the house shakes, and tongues of fire become mitres. The old garden blazes with summer, which is not officially here. Pale-yellow irises, immense red poppies. The white cat hiding from the sun. Jean's horses swigging at the water-trough. Mr Cousins's bees and Tom's aeroplane buzzing around. Myself languid in the heat, and surrounded by Laurie Lee's books – I am supposed to be celebrating his centenary.

He is walking in Spain, just before the civil war. He carries a violin, and is 18, and penniless, joyful, and naïve. His life tumbles around me on the grass. Tumultuous birdsong. Cool aspen music. I planted these tremendous trees 40 years ago, and they have shot up so they can see what is going on over the hill. All the windows are open wide. The wavy pintiled roof sheds mossy cushions. The TV aerial glitters. In a brief silence, when the birds take a break, I catch bell-ringers' practice at Little Horkesley.

The garden is a kind of unintentional botany of autographs, of stolen cuttings, inherited plantings, and remembered species. Sometimes, the giver's name comes to mind, but not the plant. It has two heydays: spring bulbs, and this midsummer splendour.

The old farmhouse is, at this moment, nothing more than a prop to hold up foliage. It smells inside and out of mint and

73

freshly shorn grass. Butterflies have to be rescued from double glazing, and the occasional swallow from my bedroom.

I preach on the moment when not only tongues of fire blazed on heads, but all languages were understood. St Luke's Acts of the Apostles has always enthralled me with its heat and voyagings, its insistence that the followers of Jesus should take to the road or the sea, and not remain a small Palestinian sect.

Of course, there were those who never left home but covered the ground mentally. It is what I am doing now, I tell Laurie Lee. I glimpsed him once when I was young. A friend said: 'You see that man at the bar – that's Laurie Lee.' He had walked all the way from Gloucestershire into fame. In *Cider With Rosie* – a great walk book – he describes it quite dangerously; for even now, all this time since, it is enough to make one pack a haversack and take to the road. Only it is best to be about 20 for it to make sense.

A friend starts up the mower. It vies with the bees. The horses toss their manes. David is having his funeral in the church, a Thomas Hardy figure from the last of the old farmworking race. He and his wife sat at the back of the church for always. A long weariness claimed him, wore him out.

The psalms understood such physical exhaustion. 'Forsake me not, O God, in my old age.' Although, wonderfully, the older one gets, the closer God is, it often seems. But, with the passing of men such as David, the gradual disappearance of those whose bodies shaped the village fields, and whose faces met the village weather in all its moods, rural life in its classic shape is concluded.

He was cremated – a hurrying of his body into dust, and different tongues of fire to claim it. The church was full to overflowing for him.

Voices of unseen riders converse as they pass the garden, and there is a slight stumbling of hoofs.

Kilvert climbs Cader Idris

TO ALDEBURGH, where Peter Grimes would confess his crimes in an opera house on the shingle. And not only this, but the Suffolk coast had taken a leaf out of the Côte d'Azur, and was balmy. My friend Ian, never a man to miss an opportunity, jumped into the sea and swam several yards. I breathed in the unaccustomed warmth, and listened to the furious gulls.

It was Sunday evening, and my having taken matins at Little Horkesley that morning seemed aeons away. For this is what the sea does: takes over. Replaces what went before with its vast significance. I heard it hollering, as it were, below the balcony of my room all night.

The costly whiff of skate and haddock rose from the fishermen's huts, and the birds cried even louder. Christianity was born to this smell and noise. Galilee was 74 square miles of serenity and turbulence, where squalls blew up, or where surfaces were calm, concealing great depth. It bred a distinctive race, as seas do. As Aldeburgh does to this day. I mean, Southwold and Great Yarmouth are only a few miles north, but are they like Aldeburgh? Not remotely.

It is Songs of Praise at Mount Bures from its modest height. And all around the epitome of flower festivals. Pure Kilvert. Or so I always think. Francis Kilvert died in 1879, and his niece Miss Kilvert was my Suffolk neighbour. The contingencies of human existence can be unbelievable. This is the time of year when I might include some of Kilvert's diary in a sermon. Might he not console others as he consoles me? St Paul blessed the Romans via the God of patience and consolation.

On a June morning such as this, Kilvert let himself out of the Golden Lion Hotel at Dolgellau to visit real lions; for the menagerie had come to town. It was 5.30 a.m., and the lions, ostriches, gnus, and antelopes, wide awake but caged up, were 'eliciting divers roars, groans, howls, hoots and grunts'. All that

I heard when at this hour I braved the sopping wet grass were Jean's horses cropping and breathing, and the final notes of the dawn chorus.

Kilvert climbed Cader Idris; I became waist-high in my wildflower meadow and sticky with pollen. But the early-ness of being outside was just the same for both of us. Only he ran into Welsh rain, and I into the clarity of an East Anglian morning. Kilvert descended Cader Idris by the 'Fox's Path', as I had done, a hundred years later.

I came into a stingy breakfast, being too idle to cook. And now, wet-footed, I am writing this, consoled by the selfish thought that never in my life have I ever had to catch the commuter's train. Only to stumble from bed to meadow at an unearthly hour. For 5.30 a.m. can be paradisal, whatever the weather.

Kilvert, a mighty walker, met early risers of all ages; whereas I meet fewer and fewer fellow tramps. Sunday afternoons might bring one or two of them out. Old paths are grown over, old views no longer seen – such as that from which, at a certain point, one can just make out Wormingford Church, or an oak which is contemporary with Shakespeare.

So back to Songs of Praise, and what to say between these hymns. And to hear them sung eloquently inside the thick old walls. George Herbert, of course. J. M. Neale, of course. Charles Wesley always consolingly brilliant.

John Clare in Poets' Corner

To Westminster Abbey to lay a wreath in Poets' Corner. It is 150 years since John Clare died. Those of us who usually meet to remember him in Helpston, his epicentre, have come to London to think of him. He actually stood on this spot, brought to it by an artist friend, and wearing his green suit. Gradually over the years he has been recognized as England's 'rural voice'. If our countryside could speak, it would be in his voice.

Dean Michael Mayne, Ted Hughes the Poet Laureate, and myself put Clare's name up here, next to Matthew Arnold's, this being the only vacant space. Later candidates would have to be inscribed on a window.

I often stayed with the Maynes at Westminster, and remember our late-night strolls in the Abbey, then empty and barely lit. A quite different place from the tourist-thronged building of the daytime. Or even of the services.

National voices casually conversed with us. I could hear Caxton's printers turning in their sleep. Now John Clare, released from madness, could speak in the marvellously sane language of his poetry to worshipper and sightseer alike for ever and ever, amen.

Ted Hughes had read Clare's perfect 'The Nightingale's Nest', in which vision and natural history meet so memorably.

Up this green woodland – ride let's softly rove,
And list the nightingale – she dwells just here.
Hush! let the wood-gate softly clap, for fear
The noise might drive her from her home of love;
For here I've heard her many a merry year –
At morn, at eve, nay, all the live-long day,
As though she lived on song. This very spot.

Or when in town in Berkeley Square. And I had given the lecture and come up from Suffolk, and Ted from Devon, and again there was this memorable sense of brief transition in which every minute counted. But nightingales like thickets and they might be rather trimmed in the West End. John Clare, being as much naturalist as poet, understood nightingale territory perfectly. My blackberry clumps are part of it.

Once I tried to follow its song via the words, and the music in the *Field Guide to the Birds of Britain and Europe*. They went like this:

> A liquid *wheet*, a loud *tac*, a soft, very short *tuc*, and a harsh kerr of alarm. His song is rich, loud, and musical, each note rapidly repeated several times; most characteristic notes, a deep bubbling *chook-chook-chook* and a slow *piu, piu, piu* rising to a brilliant crescendo.

As with John Clare's Helpston nightingale, it could be skulking and solitary. While John Keats's sang immortally, his sang ornithologically, 'Lost in a wilderness of listening leaves', aware of danger. Only, mercifully, this is nothing like that of the bird-nesting boys of my youth. 'We will only take one.' I would watch, broken-heartedly, the ritual pricking and blowing, the spurt of white and yoke in the May sun. The frail shell added to the collection.

Flower festivals loom. First Chelsea, then Wormingford. Every approach to Wormingford begs the driver to stop at the church, else we won't be able to pay the Quota.

The Cloud of Unknowing

AND so at last it arrived, the warmth. It entered the trees and the rooms, it burst the lilacs, and turned the white cat upside-down. On the evening of its coming, I mowed the long walk until I could no longer see, just feel the bliss of it. I could hear badgers snuffling and grunting, bark creaking, and late birds settling. It was too good to go in.

The other day, digging about, I exhumed an eighteenth-century pistol, its trigger cocked in the rust, a shred of its oaken butt intact. So, when my friend from the British Museum came to lunch, there was something worthy of his glance. He picked it up gingerly, and we heard it going off in *c.*1750. So what was a farmer doing with such a weapon? I was making the runner-bean wigwam when it turned up, bold as brass, a duelling gun. Red rust now, not red blood.

In church, we had heard two lessons which spoke of singing trees, and of the redeemed singing a new song. I preached on being young in Vézelay ages ago, and singing in the lovely basilica on the hilltop on Ascension Day, while the hirondelles swooped around crying, and a youth cooled the flagstones with a watering can.

Later, I looked through the gate of a garden where Colette's mother, the peerless Sido, had taught her daughter to plant and sow, smell and gather. And all the time there was this Ascension warmth and song. I had sat all noontime on the wall that secured Vézelay to its hill, gossiping with some Jesuit students and staring over Burgundy. The past is so obliging. It offers itself in digestible amounts.

In church, they sang *Aeterne Rex altissime*, in which angels will 'tremble when they see how changed is our humanity'. Like the gun from the bean bed, what comes to light is fragmental, yet shapely.

Among the first words of Acts are: 'And when he had spoken these things, while they beheld, he was taken up and a cloud received him out of their sight.' This is the cloud of unknowing. An unknown author wrote a whole book about it in the Middle Ages. He describes what he calls 'the blind stirring of love', and of 'hearing the happy music of the blessed'. He also tells us to take care not to put a cloud of forgetting between us and the natural world. And he doesn't mean dementia. He means sloth. He takes us to task.

'Do not think that the cloud I am telling you about is the sort of cloud you see in the sky or the kind of darkness you know at home when the light is out . . . By darkness I mean a lack of unknowing between you and God.' The unknown – and fascinating – writer is dealing with visions of both the natural and mystical universe. It is St Paul's misty Roman glass.

Never so many fields of rape. The world is Van Gogh from horizon to horizon. The long rains have made it very tall, and extra yellow. Skylarks mount from hidden barenesses inside it. And never such wildflowers open to the sun. The Lower Bottoms, filled with little swollen streams, are another yellow.

And then, of course, there is the may – dense, dizzy-making, sumptuous, and mind-blowing. Grandmother wouldn't have it in the house. Or lilac ('lalocs'). Big pots of it stand in the ancient kitchen to cense it. To make me think of Walt Whitman's poem.

Farmhouse Guests

DUNCAN and I agree: it is a growing year. Things grow every year, of course, but not as they do in a growing year. The garden has shot up, gone skyward. Roses look down at me, as indeed does the white cat, who is either under a hank of cool grass, or dizzily aloft in a pear tree, taking stock of the universe. A cuckoo is not far off, its cry not yet doubling.

Quiet, empty churches relax after strenuous attempts to define the Trinity. Once-a-week friends come out like birds from clocks, and we say more or less the same things. Wimbledon and atrocity take turns on the television. The one so perfect, the other so wicked. Humanity is an enigma, capable of the best and the worst. What Christ must have seen before it saw him!

We sing 'Holy, holy, holy', and, as always, I think of Reginald Heber, poet and bishop, who died young in India, after three years 'crowded with toil', nursing the sick soldiers who were on the ship. The Church seems to have insisted on this missionary enterprise when Heber would have rather stayed at home in Hodnet, Shropshire, described by Leyland as neither town nor village.

When Heber was there, it had a rectory at one end, and a prison at the other. He fulfilled the requirements of a Victorian cleric by being well-born, selfless, and a victim of work. His Trinity hymn distances God, places him beyond mortal comprehension. Our few voices rise and fall.

Later, the car creeps down the ancient farm-track, caressed by overgrowth, disturbing bees, coming to a stop where the fruit trees begin. And now, as somebody wrote, the long, long Sundays of Trinity, neither feast-day nor fast.

Twice this week, birds have flown into the house – a robin and a wren – and beat against the windows, rushing from one to the other, shocked by looking out of glass and not being able to fly through it. I cup them in my hands, and they tremble; I carry them to the door, and the release is nearly as wonderful for me as it is for them.

The white cat, who either through sloth or being well-fed, has never eaten anything which doesn't come out of a tin, adds to their terror by just gazing at them. Old houses in the middle of nowhere are open houses to butterflies, harvest mice, and, once, a toad who liked a cool brick floor. At night, I sometimes hear a squirrel, but no rats. A man from the ministry did with these long ago.

But I have always been conscious of residents other than humanity who give this address, and whose claim for shelter is historic. Moths matriculate in undrawn curtains, and spiders make a new web where I have brushed down the old one. When I was a boy, I would lie in bed and listen to a spider on a route-march on wallpaper which had come adrift, tap-tap-tapping in the dark. And the beams would give a little groan, worn out with having to hold up tons of house.

The south wall, laden with grapes, is now three feet in the ground, its orange bricks and pale beams interlocked in a kind of supportive marriage. Ancient buildings are like this, out of kilter, and the stronger for it. There is a lesson here. But the wide floorboards under the fitted carpet pine for bare feet.

To some creatures, these 'funny old places' are both home and trap.

JULY

Thomas Hardy

CATCHING Thomas Hardy's name on the News – something about building opposite Max Gate – returned me to Dorchester. I had been helping to edit the New Wessex Edition of his works, and the kind woman who now lived in the great writer's house invited me to see it. Others, including Virginia Woolf, had seen fit to mock it, but I found it perfect.

Few houses had been so adequately designed to contain a literary spirit. Hardy's brother had built it for him, unearthing Roman graves in the process. *Tess* and all the other great novels drew sightseers to it from the very start; so a barrier of conifers was planted to hide it. Conifers, being what they are, did more than what was required of them, creating a sadness; and Hardy would sometimes stand at the iron gate in the evening, longing for a visitor.

But what particularly enthralled me, as I was taken from polished room to polished room, was the quiet contained time of their clocks. I was taken back to my childhood in Suffolk, where there were old houses without radios, only the tick-tock of a fine clock. No other sound. And, of course, in Hardy's case, and in such a modest dwelling, the chatter and singing of servants. He wrote *The Dynasts* to their merriment as they played ring-board below.

Bottengoms Farm is lucky to hear church bells, and fortunate to exist beyond traffic. The great heat has revved up the dawn chorus. With the windows wide at five in the morning, I listen to a full orchestra. Then, suddenly, it stops. There is silence except for the ticking of a clock, measured: a many-wheeled heartbeat to tell that the ancient interior still breathes. Now and then an old beam catches its breath, and there is a sharp retort. A momentarily trapped bird beats against the glass; a butterfly wanders on a wall.

Giving my annual lecture to the John Clare Society, I tell my favourite time chestnut. Dumas rushes from his study to cry, 'I have finished *The Three Musketeers*!'

'But dinner won't be ready for another hour,' his wife says.

So he goes back in and starts *The Black Tulip*.

But, as the Preacher says, there is a time for everything. How I love it when he tells me that 'a dream cometh through a multitude of business'. The heatwave will have them nodding in the City, and wilting in white shirts. The Wren churches will be cool, the Thames on the boil. The cars will be burning; the pigeons will seek fountains. My aspens, like Hardy's firs, present a forest to the sun. And a whispering concerto to me.

I lie below them, putting on a show of 'business', but dreaming away. I have to preach to the Readers at the Cathedral, but not until Saturday; and to the parish, but not until Sunday. For every service there is a season.

The white cat stirs in the cool grass. For every noon, there is Whiskas. For every late July, there is Jonathan to cut the track, to fell the tall grasses and thistles, and to slice off the rise between the ruts. In July, I ceaselessly let myself out, as it were.

Not that, like Hardy, I fenced myself in, for I have done little or no planting. My growth simply comes up of its own accord, and to its own luxurious timing. Every summer without fail for centuries, creating luxuriance, idleness, and this heavy silence. What business has work at such a moment? But I must prop the tomatoes up. I have to make what Solomon called a dinner of herbs.

Incense and Mr Rix's Onions

'THE hunt will be coming by on Monday,' Stephen says. I do not tell the white cat. Sufficient unto the day, etc. It makes her tremble all over – the very sound of it.

My old friend from the British Museum comes to matins. I am to show him the Earls of Oxford's tombs in St Stephen's Chapel – Countesses, too – all in alabaster state, although their dust is elsewhere. Their name is de Vere – boar. Before this, I take matins at Little Horkesley, where those who sang to God in the Middle Ages sleep beneath our feet. Dust, dust. And angel voices ever singing. And the long, long days of Trinity, neither feast-day nor fast.

I preach on 'Brother Nature', having witnessed quite suddenly our stripped fields, not having heard so much as a far combine humming to the sky. In 1225 (when the Earls of Oxford were setting the carvers to work on their tombs), St Francis, a different kind of patrician, sat in his Assisi garden and wrote a hymn to nature, calling it 'Brother Sun and his Creatures', as he related himself to the natural world.

His family tree was the oak or ash or dark cypress. He was brother to the flowers, to the birds, to the hares. Like his Lord, Francis had moved away from the concept of the natural world's being a larder for the benefit of humanity to the concept of its being a related family.

Inherent in Christ's experience of his countryside is his wonder and delight in it. The crops, the blooms, the scenery, the creatures. He was much outside all his life, now and then complainingly so. He picks and chews corn as he walks, and as we did as Suffolk children. We ate fresh hawthorn buds, and called them bread and cheese. We gnawed raw carrots. We were the inheritors of glut when it came to fallen plums. We pretended to enjoy crab apples.

Best of all, we drank from the spring waters, a hilly meadow stream near our home, and paddled in them, our white feet startling tiny fish.

All this came to mind when I reached up to feel if my Victorias were ready. Just about. And the greengages – pick now! Aiden keeps the late-summer grass in order, and will shortly scythe the seedy overgrowth. After which the nuts will fall – what the birds have left of them. Cherry trees pale before St Stephen's Chapel, where the Earls sleep. Drizzle masks the famous view. Duncan's white barn guides me to Bottengoms Farm, from here no more than a smudge.

I am standing where the teenage Edmund stood for his coronation. It was Christmas Day. And they had all climbed Cuckoo Hill – singing, of course. Some carol about the Lord Jesus, and his coming into the world. After which there would have been a feast, and much kneeling to the boy God and the boy king. And incense, not Mr Rix's onions, although I rather like the way that they have scented the Stour Valley. Short-term economy has scattered it with pylons, alas.

The little river is lost in its fading summer growth, just giving a glitter here and there. The harvest fields have been raked and freshly seeded. Never a pause. Lots of duck and geese in echelon flight. According to Francis, they are my relatives. Benedicite creatures.

The poet Thomas Traherne insisted that we should want God's creation, should desire it – be greedy for it.

Afterwards at the Cricketers' Arms

TO LONDON. Such visits are increasingly rare. I am about to go when a thrush sings, or sloth raises its tempting head. But the only way to glimpse old friends – including Colin Thubron, the true traveller – is at the AGM of the Royal Society of Literature. The mid-afternoon carriage is empty. It slides past the waiting

Olympic Park, where I would like to see the re-ruralization of the Lea Valley. Liverpool Street is the usual scurrying-ant plaza.

With two hours to spare, I make my ritual crossing of Old Broad Street to say a prayer in St Botolph's, Bishopsgate, which I think of as my City church – more, I fear, because John Keats was baptized in it than for the East Anglian saint. I must mend my ways.

It is a warm afternoon, and a hundred office-workers are seated at little tables; the women pretty, the men all film stars. One of them lies asleep on the grass in his expensive suit, but with bare, dusty feet. A large tablet in the wall says: 'The tomb of Mr Davies' – who would have known Mr Pepys. But is this the way to get the economy moving? God bless idleness, conversation, the heat of the sun, the childhood of poets. Mr Davies, even.

In the taxi from Colchester station, the driver tells me that he might get home for a few days to see his family.

'Where is home?'

'Albania.'

The white cat waits for me at the bottom of the farm track. Whiskas for her, whisky for me. I read a few pages of *The Guermantes Way*, before dropping off.

> I retraced with my parents the course of the Vivonne – to that land of bubbling streams where the Duchess taught me to fish for trout and to know the names of the flowers whose red and purple clusters adorned the walls of the neighbouring gardens . . .
>
> The sky was still empty at those points where, later, were to rise Notre Dame of Paris and Notre Dame of Chartres, when on the summit of the hill of Laon the nave of its cathedral had not yet been poised, like the Ark of the Deluge on the summit of Mount Ararat, crowded with Patriarchs and Judges anxiously leaning from its windows

to see whether the wrath of God were yet appeased, carrying with it the types of the vegetation that was to multiply on the earth . . .

And especially at Bottengoms Farm, where wet weather is doing wonders for weeds and cultivated plants alike. Hollyhocks reach for the roof, tomatoes become trees. But now the July birds sing! And never such creamy plates of elder blossom. As for the nettles, they would win first prize anywhere.

I take a village funeral for Peter. His mother-in-law's favourite hymn was 'Through all the changing scenes of life'. Tate and Brady, of course. I read the Beatitudes. Peter was a train driver on the same line as the one which takes me to London, and he would have driven me, I expect. 'Make you his service your delight,' Peter. I lead him to the double grave. 'Afterwards at the Cricketers' Arms', the service sheet says.

Staverton Thicks

NOT far from the Suffolk coast there stands the fragment of an Augustinian priory, on whose walls hang 36 stone shields, which, hundreds of years ago, were full of knightly information. But rains and winds, and burning suns, have erased it, so that they are left as a *tabula rasa*, or 'the mind in its uninformed original state', as the philosopher John Locke would have said. Or as a lesson to us all, as Julian of Norwich would have added.

Nearby lies an oyster-bed. Across the road there is a dying forest, which never dies, in which a woman who had been Queen of France, and her second husband, the Duke of Suffolk, had a picnic. This forest is where oaks and hollies in terminal decay hang on to each other in everlasting life. It is so quiet that you can hear a dying leaf drop. But now and then a gaudy pheasant will kick up a din.

I used to take all my friends there – John Nash, Richard Mabey, and James Turner. John used to say that he 'liked the dead tree in the landscape'. And he sat drawing in this not-quite-dead wood for hours, while I wandered about, ducking the liana-like ivies that fell from on high, sloshing my feet through the skeletal leaves that filled the ruts, and listening hard for perhaps a nightingale. It was dreadful how the trees mounted one another, and strange how, in what seemed their last moments, they reached for the sky.

A few yards along the lane, and equally dark, stood another forest, one of rigid conifers, all standing to attention, through which the north wind whistled and the squirrels swung. St Edmund – England's Sebastian, it is rumoured – received temporary burial here. But who can say? My head is often an old picture-book with its backing gone and its pages dangling. So take no notice. Each one of us knows a few truths about our home ground – and a great many fancies.

When I was in Australia, my heart sank at the lighting of the barbecue; for the mighty feast of burnt steak, sausages, beer, and bread would take many hours. I thought of the ducal lovers, lying here on the then rich grass, eating cakes, and listening to lutes and birds, and the oaks and hollies standing quiet, and the sun having room to blaze. And the great armorial on the priory being a great read, and fully coloured. And the seagulls sailing about.

And King Henry VIII, the Duchess's brother, full of rage in London; for she had no right to marry her beloved Duke without his permission – she who had been Queen of France. What could Henry do? How dare they present him with a *fait accompli*? So he sentenced them to stay in Suffolk for ever.

I like to look at the Duchess's tomb when I am in Bury St Edmunds. It is tucked into a corner of St Mary's, and, unlike the armorial of the knights, it is wonderfully readable still.

Once, when the tomb was being mended, they found hanks of Tudor-red hair. And this lady somehow makes me think of Queen Esther and the Grand Vizier Haman, although they do not share the faintest resemblance. You see how unreliable and fanciful I am.

We could go to the picnic place this afternoon. Why not?

James the Prison Chaplain

'WHAT', enquires Sir John, after the service, 'is "the Proper"?' I explain, and we all go home little the wiser. It is St Swithun's, and the sun stares down on us. Lunch in the wet-but-warm garden, and kindly joined by the white cat. Yesterday, we travelled 100 miles to Helpston to honour John Clare, our natural-history poet *sans* peer, and I gave my 31st presidential address in the marquee.

We went to the Blue Bell, the pub where he worked as a youth, doubling the professions of ploughman and potman. Morris dancers clicked and cried in the car park. Schoolchildren had placed 'midsummer cushions' round Clare's grave. These are made by sticking wildflower heads into turf. Clare wrote about what I call his 'commonwealth of flowers'.

The most terrible thing for him during his long asylum years was the deprivation of the seasonal countryside, for, like all village people, his interior clock kept time with that of the birds and plants. He complained to a friend:

> Like the caged Starnel of Sterne, I can't get out . . .
>
> I love the rippling brook and the singing of birds. But I can't get out to see them or hear them – while other people are looking at gay flower gardens. I love to see the quaking bull rushes and the broad lakes in the green meadows, and

the sheep tracks over a fallow field, and a land of thistles in flower . . . I am in this damned madhouse and can't get out.

James, the chaplain of Chelmsford Prison, comes to evening prayer with us, fresh from the myriad troubles of men who deservedly yet tragically can't get out. As a nation, we are notorious for locking people up and forgetting them. George Fox could never forget the teenaged James Parnell, who had walked all the way to Carlisle to be converted by him and made a member of the Society of Friends, and who was now thrown into prison in Colchester to be slowly murdered by the gaoler's wife. So Fox visited him.

Jesus said that when we visit someone in prison we visit him. We can visit prisoners by not forgetting that they exist. The demented are now prisoners in the old people's home. How can they be visited? Clare's madness never sounds very mad to me. A multiplicity of difficulties had brought him down. A couple of signatures had confined him for ever. Except that his poems ran free.

Clare's feelings towards flowers were intimate and profound, and not unlike those of a child who runs towards them. He and his friend Tom Porter 'used to go out on Sundays to hunt curious wild flowers'. And when he was 'down', he would write to Mr Henderson, Lord Fitzwilliam's head gardener, to ask him to bring him both cultivated and uncultivated flowers. They grew side by side in Clare's own garden.

For the poet, botany became part of both his humanity and his theology. They had rarity, but not rank. He would write compulsively about them, in and out of his 'prison'.

Thirty years ago, it was chemical sprays which threatened our wildflowers. Now it is the lawnmower. Stripes are part of our worship. Clare taught his neighbours what to find in the ruts. Such stamped-on treasures!

John Clare with Herdboys and Girls

A CLEAR day. Not empty day. The difference should be, well, clear. Nobody is coming, the diary says. Give yourself a break from the new book, my head says. The skies concur. Venus having wandered across the sun, cloud Alps promise downpours as contrition. Even planets should know their place.

All this rain. The garden grows a foot an hour. I cut bamboo poles for the runner-bean wigwam, trim their tops, and arrange them in a circle. Bamboo is a kind of grass. A huge stand of it gives monumental importance to a little lawn. The July birds sing their heads off. They, too, celebrate a clear day.

What did John Clare do on a clear day? Slip from sight of his nosey neighbours, for one thing. Steal away to the open-cast quarry down the road, where no one in his right mind would want to go, there to lie flat and let his imagination do all the work. Out of sight, out of mind. Why were they all so interested in him?

The father of an Ipswich Town footballer told me how his son could not go out because of the staring. His boy would have to drive to some foreign city, like Norwich, if he wanted to avoid all those eyes. Touches, even.

John Clare walked away to the wilds to converse 'with shepherds and herdboys', to learn the fiddle from Gypsies, and to find a clear day. William Hazlitt, when he was a boy, heard them calling from the Manse, but laid low in the long grass, not answering. There was reading to be done. I did this when I was 12, feeling wicked.

The rain-growth of the past few days reminds me of all this, the shelter, the English countryside out of control, the kitchen garden pleading to be sticked, the grey puddles, the clouds sailing over their surface. A nervous green woodpecker has just stopped its dipping flight to rest for seconds, a yard from the window. Hares are about, they say.

'When are you going to get Jonathan to cut the sides of your track?' they say.

'When it stops,' I say.

The rain. Every now and then it drops like a curtain on the scene. The white cat trots in like a walking dishcloth to dry herself on my jersey. It is murky for a clear day. But soft, I'll give it that. And sweetly scented, like Shakespeare's bank. Church-tower flints look like crown jewels from so much wet polishing, and last week's bunting like sad rags.

It was on such a day as this that the youthful John Clare went out hoping to see some girls' legs. But they had lengthened their skirts to hide their muddy stockings. Such is life. He noted 'signs of the weather in animals'.

> Cats eat grass and their eyes lose their brightness. Swallows gather in company. Quails make more chirpings. Fowls go to roost more early. Dogs turn sick. Frogs turn black, and gather round their homes. Horses play around the yard. Hogs champ . . . cattle toss molehills. Animals sport and play before a storm. Cows bellow.

And poets who see that it is far too wet to work in the fields cry hurrah! Now for a dry spot in the Hills and Holes, the abandoned quarry, where one can read and write, dream and fade from sight.

Omar Khayyám in Suffolk

HAVING preached on St Mary Magdalene at matins, I returned home to find three Persian poets in the garden. Having told my young neighbours that I once lived near Boulge, the Suffolk village where Edward FitzGerald translated *The Rubáiyát of Omar Khayyám*, they had driven to his grave and recited what was once one of the most popular poems in the English language. I knew most of it by heart in my teens. Published in 1859, it was found in a bookseller's tuppenny box by Swinburne, and soon everyone was reciting it aloud.

And now, having in my vague way mentioned this famous tale to friends up the lane, here they are, princes from the East, exotic and beautiful, and waiting for a lunchtime drink. Worse or better, whichever you prefer, they returned to their London flats in those clothes. I simply hung my cassock on a peg.

But the Bottengoms roses in their innocence and profusion perfumed the whole garden. The white cat observed all this with some disdain, sprawling on the bone-dry earth and looking up with little interest. Give her good plain human behaviour any day. One of the boys had actually visited Omar's city, seen his rose *in situ*, slept under his stars. On the strength of this, he returned to his London flat in his robe, sash and sandals.

Then John the Vicar calls to discuss 4 August, that tragic date. He has chosen Thomas Hardy's 'Men who March Away', and Rupert Brooke's 'The Soldier' and 'Safety' for me to read. The latter is a little-known poem about the safety of death. 'Safe shall be my going.' So let the slaughter begin.

Time does not still the madness of the First World War. My teenage father ran from the plough to the recruiting station at Stowmarket, and was soon at Gallipoli. Brooke was on the same convoy, but a mosquito intervened, and the troopship pulled in to Skyros, where a grave was dug with difficulty on the rocky shore. Men who sail away.

I lent his poems to Edward, the young friend in the Omar costume, grateful to him for having recreated and freshened what I had thought of as a conventional literary experience.

There comes a time when what was everybody's 'read' is nobody's read. Also – I speak for myself – when the Booker Prize list is full of well-known names of which one has never heard. I was a Booker Prize judge, years ago. I rose at six every day, and read and read. On the doorstep, when it was warm enough. A fine cat who now sleeps in the wood sat beside me.

We gave the prize to William Golding for his amazing sail to Botany Bay, *Rites of Passage*, a novel in which the passenger list gives little away. He looked like an old sea captain himself, blue-eyed and bristly. I thought of St Paul when he offered to be thrown overboard, *en route* to Rome.

Seafaring was as risky as skyfaring. 'But then,' as a philosophical old friend once said, 'if you didn't take risks, you wouldn't go anywhere.'

It is bliss, now, not to go far. To stay in the summer garden. To pack the passport away. To pray. To think of what to say on Trinity 7. It is Samuel, of course, Samuel the kingmaker. The little boy who heard God's voice in the night. 'I am here, Lord.' The little boy who would go far.

Books bake on the lawn, their leaves turned by warm winds. Beyond the garden, onions for the supermarket are irrigated by dazzling jets. It is full summer.

Jon Edgar brings my Bust

THE current shelling of an Eastern city brings Milton's *Samson Agonistes* into my head. 'Eyeless in Gaza, at the mill with slaves.' The heroic leader has been seduced, cropped, blinded, but in a moment of God-given return of strength, he is able to pull the house down on his tormentors.

An apologist for the bombing is unable to persuade me or anyone else of its righteousness. Milton's Samson is not named on the breakfast news, but when 'Gaza' is said, he seems to criticize the military action taken against a modern city in which today's children cower in their classrooms. Hasn't the world seen enough of this 'justified' response? Words would have done. Words would have done for all wars.

Apart from Gaza, the radio says that the summer will break today. Though little sign of it as yet. The ancient farmhouse continues to bake; the wasps hang around. Climbing roses burst against the warm walls. My freshly scythed orchard turns into hay. At 6 a.m., the garden is sopping wet and cold to bare feet, as I carry yesterday's letters to the box for the postman.

This is the day when the clay-sculptor Jon Edgar delivers my bust. He carries it through the tall plants, and here I am in three dimensions, and as I have not known myself before. If only Charles I could have seen his head in the round, what might our history have been!

My question now is, where shall my head be put? Think of the white cat. Think of some sudden movement. Clay heads are as fragile as bone heads. But Jon soon discovers a place from which it can survey the universe safely. After which we drive to Mount Bures for a celebratory fish and chips and beer.

By this time, the sun knows no limits. I tell Jon about the Iron Age folk sleeping beneath our feet, and about the Mount being all of 30 feet high. After lunch, we visit the soaring door-angels at Stoke-by-Nayland; silvery with centuries, they rise to a Virgin that the Reformers could do little about, considering the cost of new doors.

The day becomes hotter and hotter, and the passing cornfields more and more golden. Not a soul about. If you want outsiders, you must go to Ambridge. A church-size combine presses us into the blackberries *en-passant*. Hollyhocks loom. Pigeons play last-across. Irrigation jets play Versailles. 'There's a lot going on,' we tell each other. We mean for an English village in late July. We might even see a man at work.

Trinity 6, and we are to remember a holy family who fed and lodged the Lord as he walked the rough roads in the heat. Two sisters and their brother remain the founders of Christian hospitality. George Herbert would find Jesus at the 'ordinary' table in the inn. I can remember the 'farmers' ordinary' in a small Suffolk town when I was a boy. It was kept by two sisters, and the farmers walked across from the corn exchange on market day to eat roast beef, whatever the temperature. None of your silly salads.

Plaster labourers lolled against plaster sheaves above the corn exchange in attitudes of what the Book of Common Prayer calls 'plenty'. The corn exchange is now the public library, but still they loll in the full sun, sickles at the ready. The mere ghost of agriculture haunts our country towns, and heatwaves seem to draw it out. What shall we sing at matins? 'With prosperous times our cities crown, Our fields with plenteousness.'

AUGUST

Women Bishops?

THE peerless August goes its way: day after day of sunshine, the garden heavy with scents, the churches, too. St Paul tells us 'not to murmur'; the News tells us ghastly things. In his Diary, Francis Kilvert tells me what he did on an August day a century-and-a-half ago. He is the 32-year-old curate of Langley Burrell, Wiltshire – a strong, handsome young man who would die before he was 40, suddenly, from peritonitis. The floral arches for his wedding served for his funeral.

So how could I possibly murmur, given so many years, so many summers? In fact, having to go to London to talk after a literary lunch, I grew quite scolding, myself and the elderly audience having been awarded all these summers, and doing anything but sing the Benedicite.

But then there comes August weeding. Searching for something to complain about, we look at the towering plants that have taken over the flowerbeds. How have they usurped them without our seeing them before they were splendid in their own right, and too good for the chop?

I find myself apologizing for them to visitors, the wicked balsam in particular. Then I find an enthusiastic note on it in the matchless *Victorian Dictionary of Gardening*, edited by none other than the Director of Kew, and I must quote it in order that anyone afflicted by the current abuse of certain specimens should find heart.

This is how our ancestors saw balsam: 'It is one of the showiest of summer and autumn flowers, and well deserves a place in every garden. Although of comparatively easy cultivation, good blossoms . . . are far too rarely seen. A good Balsam flower should be quite as double as a perfect Camellia.'

Sitting among my balsam, their seeds peppering me, and the white cat sound asleep at their roots, I say to myself that August wouldn't be August without them.

A different firing, that of August 1914, fills the commemorative radio programmes. To the young, the First World War must sound like the Crimea. But, in church, an old man listens to his great-uncles' names being read aloud, and, shaking hands with him after the service, I am astonished and moved to see that his eyes are full of tears.

At dinner, we hazard guesses at which of our women deans – or, indeed, curates – might become women bishops. And what would Mrs Proudie have said? Or indeed Barbara Pym? It is fatal to take one of her novels out into the sun on a day like this. Nothing else will be done for hours. There should be a special place in the order of blessedness of those who take us into realms of delight via idleness, as reading is often called. 'They tell me that life is the thing,' remarked a young American long ago, 'but I prefer reading.'

There is a big chair in our departed village school, now closed down, where anyone is invited to just – read. Perhaps nothing in the history of mankind has produced so much happiness as reading. Ordered to bed when we were children, we would plead: 'Oh, Mum, just this last chapter.'

Now and then I think – and not at all dismally – just to read this summer, because it seems enough. Faith brings its own philosophy. It structures time. At this minute, two men are abseiling across the face of Big Ben, giving it a wipe. It is made of thin glass. The fragility of our existence!

The Caretakers

MID August. Mr Cousins's bees are rifling my flowers in the late afternoons of hot days. Distant throbs betray a combine harvester, the first machine in the field. Barely a bird. Just this still warmth and motionless skies. Bell-ringing practice to go with so many bell-shaped blooms. I imagine Barry calling the tune.

Just a handful of neighbours maintain the three churches, change their frontals, Hoover their carpets, polish their brass, unlock, lock up, count the candles, turn the pages of the visitors' books. Turn the pages, too, of the dead.

Immensely grand folk sleep here and there, nodding away until Kingdom come. Here is Jane Austen's cousin or aunt from Chawton. How did she get to Little Horkesley? Someone will know. Here are John Constable's uncles from Wormingford mill, with a confident Esq.

Here is the poor young man who apologized to me for wearing a hat in church, cancer having robbed him of his hair. Here is beloved Gordon, who survived the Western desert and was photographed with Monty. Here is John Nash, who painted the Stour valley all his days. Here, making sharp corners for the tower, are Roman bricks, warm to the touch still. Here are noticeboards naming a vanished vicar, or rector. Here is summer weather. I sit on a burning bench and thank God for it.

In Swann's Way an old man tells a young man:

> In my heart of hearts, I care for nothing in the world now but a few churches, books – two or three, pictures – rather more, perhaps, and the light of the moon when the fresh breeze of youth (such as yours) wafts to my nostrils the scent of gardens whose flowers my old eyes are not sharp enough, now, to distinguish.

Mercifully, I see not only the confident bell-shaped blooms of August, but the insects that rock them. How active the month is! Although, personally speaking, I have to admit that torpor reigns. Only those whose names on tombs remind me of their old busyness are less active than I.

Squinting through my lashes, I think I can pick out the blue smudge of hill on which they crowned Edmund, king and martyr, on Christmas Day, long ago. What else happened round about 860? Well, the convolvulus would have rioted in August, sure as fate. And the mother of the Lord would be high in the sacred firmament. And the husbandmen would be sharpening their sickles, or just lolling about in the sun.

And the mindless taking of life by the raiders, just like that by the Cairo authorities at the moment, would have been going on here and there in the name of government. Or possibly not. And possibly some enchanting seasonal sloth, with the August sun on one's neck, and a slowdown in one's heart, it being too soon to gather anything except pollen.

They say that Edmund would have been about 30 – which is far too soon to die. Morons stripped him, tied him to a tree, and made him into a target. This mindless taking of life and rattling of weapons – in August!

I think that my *Garrya elliptica* is on its last legs. Named after Michael Garry, of the Hudson Bay Company, it is propping up yards of grapevine. But if you chop it down it will rise again. A neighbouring holly says: 'Yes, yes! Give me more light.' But the white cat says: 'Let it be.'

The Tye

I AM surrounded by tyes and teys. Nedging Tye, Marks Tey, Bulmer Tye, Cuckoo Tye, where Father came from. They are native to north Essex and west Suffolk, and they began as pastures that were a good way from the main village, but which often grew a farmhouse or some stranded cottages.

Bottengoms Farm is a kind of tye. It grew up along the parish boundary line of Wormingford and Little Horkesley, and would have spent most of its centuries hearing and seeing very little of what went on in them. It would have been a two-mile walk to church in their case. But, with the wind in their favour, one could have listened to the bells.

There is a soft western wind at this moment. It caresses the old walls, and stirs the aspens, making quite a noise. Almost nobody walks here any more. Maybe with the dog, late on Sunday afternoons. They are harvesting; but where? A combine hums from different directions, but there is no Indian fire-like dust to say where.

West winds are luxurious, like the great fans that disturbed the Egyptian air for Prince Joseph, and I have a good mind to sit outside and read *No Name* by Wilkie Collins. But it gets harder and harder to do nothing, with East Anglian puritanism in one's blood. Polly comes to remind me of the Suffolk Poetry Society meeting.

The lectionary says: 'Don't forget Sunday.' What happens then? It is all answers. Will the west wind last to blow across the oaken knight and his wives? To carry the butterflies and dragonflies towards the bees as they rock in the balsam?

David arrives to say goodbye before he goes flower-hunting in Pretoria. These friends, how they get about! He attends, now and then, the spiritualist church, which makes me think of Madame Arcati. His real spiritualism is with plants. He can always say what flowers there are beneath his feet.

We have some red wine, and talk of wetlands. The owls have been crying – the little owls, which live along the farm track, and which were once called jillyhooters.

Last Sunday, Stephen and I went a dozen miles downriver to Flatford Mill, where it was a family occasion. Youthful fathers and mothers and broods in boats. Or sitting in the bird garden. Or pointing to living Constables. The great artist, who lived in Hampstead, once wrote to his brother Abram the miller, asking him if it would be all right if he brought his seven children to Flatford Mill for a holiday. Abram said: 'Certainly, if you wish to have them all drowned.'

Locks and mill races are deep and treacherous. The young fathers were holding the hands of their boys and girls tight as they strolled the footpaths. The west wind here provides a descant to the perpetual roar of deep water. A woman is painting a Constable on an easel. The river weeds are rocking with insects. Nothing is still.

But tomorrow is Sunday. Wormingford matins. Little Horkesley's farm-walk. No peace for the wicked. And 2 Peter – so beautiful: 'My children, love must not be a matter of words or talk; it must be genuine and show itself in action. This is how we may know that we belong to the realm of truth ... This letter is to assure you that you have eternal life.' I preach on Caedmon the herdsman and his hymn.

Wilkie Collins in Aldeburgh

'FOR, lo, the winter is past, the rain is over and gone,' Brian reads, bringing me up with a start, for these are the words I had carved on John Nash's tombstone. But lichen is eating them up. Not that the artist would have minded. His gardening friend brought a great spray of blossom to his funeral, but took it back home afterwards.

These rites soon become fragmentary, these graves indecipherable. It is as it should be. Massive Georgian memorials rise from the mown grass and tell us nothing. Today's marble tells us what *The Churchyards Handbook* says, little more. Hart's tongue takes refuge in the crevices of a table-tomb so that the mower won't get at it.

At Little Horkesley, I meet a teenager in a crash-helmet laying flowers on his father's neat mound. 'He was forty,' he tells me. 'So young,' I reply. 'Yes, so young,' echoes the helmet. A motorbike lolls by the hedge.

As the poets have said, a country churchyard – and in every country – is still the most contemplative spot on earth. Dust to lichen, to thought, to acceptance.

The other garden, the one with runner-beans and bedraggled roses, is drying itself out. I read *No Name* by Wilkie Collins in it, an amazing novel, set in Aldeburgh, and a lesson to us all. The parents of Magdalen and Norah have forgotten to change their will; so all the money goes to an uncle. Norah does nothing, but Magdalen does everything she can, fair and foul, to get it back.

It was written in a tall clapboarded house a few yards from the sea – and only a few steps from a little balconied cottage where Margery Sharp wrote *The Foolish Gentlewoman*. Everywhere, fugitive, compelling fiction is created. Late in the evening, I would pass Sharp's balcony and see her in the lamplight smoking a cigarette, or playing cards with her husband at a little table, the day's work done.

My day's work is far from done, and I close *No Name* with a jolt. Just because there is no one here to tell me, that doesn't mean that this is not the time to relax.

A long way off, the athletes have been strenuous, and the City negative. I turn to music. There was a time in this old farmhouse when if you wanted music, you had to sing a song. I put on Herbert Howells – the music he wrote for his little dead son. It is seriously beautiful, not so much sad as elatedly tragic. And profoundly English.

I look in the lectionary for what I have to say and do on Sunday. And think. It says Jeremy Taylor, Florence Nightingale, and the Blessed Virgin Mary. It says: 'Take your pick.' It says that the long, long Sundays of Trinity are with us at last. It says you preached on that last year. One altar candle will burn up, and the other will hardly burn at all.

But light will fall on Jane Austen's great-aunt's slab in the sanctuary. A second marriage brought her here and out of her way. Not that she would have read her niece's novels. She went too soon for that.

I plead, for the chancel-bound collection of us, God's defence, he being the author of peace.

Thoughts for Today

THOUGHT FOR THE DAY varies in its memorability. Some you catch; some you do not. Recently I caught one that recreated a summer's day, Box Brownie and all. It was about losing the nearness of Christ. Particularly in old age. To illustrate this loss, the speaker used a painting by Raphael, *The Madonna of the Pinks*. A handsome Italian woman sits for the great artist, but her son does not. Being a toddler rather than a baby at breast, he has to be kept still, and his mother achieves this by means of a flower.

Ages ago, in a Suffolk meadow, another lady arranges the four of us in a flowery meadow to take our photo. Unlike now, she poses us, a baby sister and three brothers in sailor suits, like a reduced cricket team. One of my brothers is chewing a bit of grass, and the other is, like the Lord, kept from wriggling by a bright object – a bunch of keys.

Tall August plants waver above us. A few yards away, and out of sight, there is a deep pit in which men dig clay for bricks. The men have been to the Western Front and to Gallipoli. The lady's snaps will be sent to Chester to be developed for one-and-sixpence. After the holiday, she will return to London, to our grief; for we love her, although we have long forgotten her name. But the four children go on sitting in the grass for ever, the restless one stilled.

The Lady in the Raphael picture is as close as anyone can get to the Son, and the worshippers in the darkly rich church would have come close because of her. The artist, too, was youthful and beautiful, dying at 37 on Good Friday, the same day he was born.

He was able to reveal in his work the energy that lies in stillness. His mother was heartbroken when they sent him away to be a student, to paint other mothers as the Mother of God, but keeping them human. Like Mary. When Millais painted Jesus as a lad in the carpenter's shop, with grubby feet and workworn hands, the Victorians went wild. But as they said in the synagogue after he had read the lesson so wonderfully, 'Isn't he the carpenter's son?'

And wasn't he the walker? Art tends not to show him striding out, on the move, travelling. But poetry does. One of the reasons we go to church is to catch up with him, since he is so out of sight at home. Liturgy causes us to put a spurt on, as do many 'walking' hymns. We tramp through office, garden, the drifting afternoon telly, the supermarket, the money, and he is a mere dot in the distance, far, far ahead, undiverted by what diverts us most, and strangely most out of sight when we are in the fast car or train.

The Queen in *Alice in Wonderland* says: 'Now, here, you see, it takes all the running you can do, to keep in the same place.' Religion itself keeps on the go; yet it can get us nowhere. Often, in our country churches, I talk of John Bunyan (the congregations are tolerant of my heroes), a big man with a slow step who remapped Bedfordshire for Christ and the reading world. 'Come, my Way, my Truth, my Life: Such a way as gives us breath,' wrote his near-contemporary, out of puff because of illness.

Schoolmarms and Monkey-Puzzles

AS WITH most of us, my past offers itself either as a serial that promises to run and run, or as vignettes that are complete in themselves. I am idling around the childhood market town when a VR letter-box says: 'Halt!' Two schoolmistresses are passing. They are sisters, the Miss Crossleys. They wear small hats and lisle stockings, and they carry armfuls of red exercise-books.

According to the present notion of them, suffering from a shortage of men – it is the 1930s – they will stay spinsters. But since they will lose their profession if they marry, being a teacher might be a preferred choice to that of wife. They swing along in strap shoes, and with ready smiles.

'Good morning, Miss Crossley. Good morning, Miss Crossley,' the boys and girls cry. To which Miss Crossley?

They live in the dusty shade of monkey-puzzle trees in a brick villa named after the Prince Consort. It has flashing plate-glass windows and heavy drapes, and no pupil has ever entered it.

In August, it is locked up, deserted. It is then that the Miss Crossleys go on great travels – Snowdonia, or the Wash. 'Do you think they take their tuning-fork? Their Box Brownie?'

No one has seen their snapshots, their going, or their coming back. And the monkey-puzzle villa looks the same whether it is occupied or deserted. And Mr Hurst, the postman, empties their letter box three times a day, whether they are there or not.

They smile as they swing along to the elementary school, and have low, throaty voices.

'Walk, don't run, children.'

'Yes, Miss Crossley.'

Minute sweetshops were oases on the way. Respect rather than love floated them along. It made conjecture out of the question. So what did go on in the monkey-puzzle villa out of class? Library books, ludo, prognostications. Catherine would do well; Aubrey would not. The blackboard stars foretold it.

All this was brought on by discovering a photo of the monkey-puzzle which Thomas Hardy had planted at Sturminster Newton in the autumn of 1876. And, as with the Miss Crossleys, too near the house. He and Emma were newly married, but while their unmarried servant became pregnant, she did not. He was in his early thirties, and writing *Far From the Madding Crowd*. She said: 'Your novel seems sometimes like a child, all your own and none of me.'

Thunderous weirs in the neighbourhood provided a way out, should his characters find life impossible. My childhood river was the Suffolk Stour; his the Dorset Stour. My early water-meadows had been half-flooded town-lands since the Middle Ages; his a territory for desperate remedies.

In a wet year, you might find it hard to find where our river began and its pastures ended. Enormous trees such as the monkey-puzzles, planted as striplings, threw their weight about in small streets. And, of course, in the Miss Crossleys' dry patch of massively walled-in garden.

Both here, and in Hardy's garden, they announced social confidence, light not gloom, a ground-to-sky magnificence. They rose in pairs before double villas, anything from 50 to 100 feet whose inhabitants need say no more.

'*Araucaria imbricata*, speak for us! We will put up with your everlasting Chilian dust and shade.' But Hardy and Emma moved on, until their worst tree-planting ever at Max Gate. Here the author of *The Woodlanders* planted so many pines that he could not see out. He wrote a complaining poem about this.

Earthquake

ELEGIAC days. I have been given an ash-plant walking stick that John Masefield cut from a hedge on the Western Front. He was a medical orderly. I lean on it in the peaceful August garden. The poplars sing in hushed voices. It has gained a polish where hands have held it, and a ferrule. I try it out on the long walk, and it sends up summer dust. 'Walk while ye have the light, lest darkness come upon you,' Jesus said. Excellent advice.

In church we remember 4 August 1914, first silently, with Vaughan Williams's *The Lark Ascending*, and then with touches of compline. I read Rupert Brooke's 'Safety' and 'The Soldier'. His safety lies in the indestructible heart of things. Very soon, in the same fleet as bore my teenage father to Gallipoli, a mosquito would take his life. He was 27. And here am I, old in the old garden, eating raspberries, telling tales to the white cat, thinking of what to say on Sunday.

There are celebrated dragonflies here. I forget why they are celebrated, but naturalists call on them and they sometimes enthrone themselves on my bare skin, gossamer, shimmering. 'August for flying,' they say. Roses tremble beneath them. August for the people,' W. H. Auden said. August for lazing, say I. I am no good at this, however, which is just as well, considering the state of my desk. But I adore the sounds of August, its orchestral winds, its midnight creaks, its loud birds, its noises off – i.e. the sound of other people's pleasures. And the splutter of my neighbour's little aeroplane as he takes a look at our valley.

They are harvesting here and there, not that anyone is interested. The most disturbing thing in today's farming year is the total lack of interest in the harvest. In church, Harvest Festival is a kind of apology for ignoring the fields. All is safely gathered in, the tinned peas, the outsize marrow, the magnificent flowers. And there is gratitude, of course. The appalling things we see on the evening screen make me feel lucky. And goodness itself is commonplace, or should we say ordinary?

And while we know a good deal about each other in the village, our lives are too expanded these days for us to feel that we are 'observed'. Think of John Clare, who had to hide away in order to write. But then writers are very odd people.

New Zealanders come to see me, and carrying gifts. They call the earth tremors there 'the shakes'. They are rebuilding Christchurch Cathedral, and not entirely of cardboard. The loss of the beautiful Victorian architecture four years ago brings tears to our eyes. We mention John Selwyn, who took the gospel to New Zealand, teaching himself Maori on the ship.

I tell them of my old friend Christopher Perkins, who taught at Wellington Art School, and whose work is now in the National Gallery. As a youth, I sat for him as St John, dressed in a sheet. It was for a Dorset reredos. I remember his sketchbooks, with their pages and pages of New Zealand towns and settlements, the wooden houses and tin roofs, and their sense of being far away. As far as you could go. And particularly the Scots.

They – these visitors – were on their way to Scotland, making me feel envious. It is almost the time when the Highlands' scent of heather is so seductive that it makes one long to emigrate. But the white cat says, 'Know your place.' Which I try to.

SEPTEMBER

Flying Seeds

ONE of my childhood autumn sounds was to hear a big spider negotiating the ancient bedroom wallpaper where it had become loose on the uneven wall. September spiders now appear in the bath, and have to be carried to the garden by the glass-and-postcard method. In fact, the latter spider transport is an essential September fitting, by the soap.

In the beds below, Himalayan balsam – *Impatiens glandulifera* – fires off all guns as I brush past it. It should be by the stream. If one has to have a pest, then have *Impatiens*, with its pink-purple flowers, sculptural stems, and happy bees rocking in its petal boats. I give it its head. Let it flourish where it will.

It was first discovered in the Looe Valley in 1900 and called 'a cumbersome weedy thing'. Well, so it is. But something infinitely more. It is undeniably grand and extraordinarily beautiful. When it is over, when it has aimed its last seeds and there is a hint of rot, how easy it is to pull up the shallow plate of its roots and carry it off to where it can speedily perish, its seeds popping all the way.

'Squeeze the pod gently,' I tell the little girl. The life between her fingers shocks her.

My garden is watery. Springs in all directions. And this morning, moles building an Underground, mercifully where it doesn't make me wild. So much going on, including the

Vicar's departure. We were given good notice when this would happen. In September. But September has a curious habit of being distant until it is 'here'.

Priests look down from the incumbents board. Some stayed five years, others fifty. In a village, their ministries were like rural reigns. 'In Mr Tufnell's time,' we say. Our diocese, too, has shifted about. As for deaneries – we have been here, there, and everywhere. Yet the parish itself is immovable. The same Stour-side confidence in itself, the same views – and not only the geographical ones. And now Henry is off to where he and his wife will have to work hard doing nothing. Or filling 'nothing' in with this strange commodity known as retirement. And what of us?

The Bishop is coming to see him off. He – Henry, that is – must have his last word in three separate pulpits, and in three magazines. Christian unity is all very well, but a benefice must be disunited, now and then. I met a previous incumbent the other day, and was astonished to find him well and sane after twenty years without us.

Mr Rix is irrigating his vegetable acres. A Versailles of fountains swivel in all directions. Wet sugar-beet look almost pretty. But summer is leaving us, and the early mornings are sharp. Late roses are profuse. And such cloud formations! The light in East Anglia is said to be like that of the Low Countries, and the making of Thomas Gainsborough and John Constable, and especially the Norwich school of artists. This month, it has the clarity of cut glass. Orange and grey mountains journey above our heads.

Shaking hands in the churchyard, an old friend complains of 'those halls of Sion being conjubilant with song' – 'all jubilant' would have been enough. Yet it would not, although a leaving congregation is not the moment to defend J. M. Neale.

Not a fallen leaf on the graves.

Robert Louis Stevenson's Evensong

THE day has progressed from wild beginnings to limpid sunshine; so no need to have put friends off. It leaves me, however, with the best thing ever – a day in hand.

For the white cat, it is always a day in hand. She murmurs at departing birds. Bunches of blackberries, tomatoes, and grapes hang heavily in the thinning leaves. A palaeontologist holds forth on the radio, learned and enticing. BC and AD become mere yesterdays. The years, the years!

And stony evidence of immense time in the Stour Valley, some of it fixed in the church tower and scrubbed by our weather. 'Read Wisdom,' the lectionary orders. I am reading Mrs Stevenson's introduction to her husband's prayers on Samoa, however. She called him Robert; their household called him Tusitala, storyteller.

And thus evensong. A hundred years later, I find them apt for our household the Church. The Samoans blew a war conch to summon people to prayer; but all that I can hear when I put the South Sea shell to my ear, as I did as a child, is the faraway and wonderful sounds of Pacific waves, distant yet always close. Friends' children listen to them, and are mesmerized.

'I don't think it ever occurred to us that there was any incongruity in the use of the war conch for the peaceful invitation to prayer,' Stevenson's wife wrote.

> The Samoans trooped in through all the open doors, some carrying lanterns if the evening were dark, all moving quietly, and dropping with Samoan decorum in a wide semicircle on the floor beneath the great lamp that hung from the ceiling . . . Often, we were forced to pause until the strangely savage, monotonous noise had ceased.

Poor young Robert was dying, and he like everyone else with a fresh flower daily stuck behind his ear, and the stories tumbling out of him. He wrote torrentially on anything and everything, feeling time running him into the ground. And he so young. The classic consumptive.

When I was a boy, I was taken to see a dying girl, Lily, but all I saw was her waxen loveliness. All that the Samoans heard was the Edinburgh voice running on, ravished as it was with words.

Stevenson has been ordered south.

And yet the ties that still attach him to the world are many and kindly. The sight of children has a significance for him, as it may have for the aged also, but not for others. If he has been used to feel humanely, and to look upon life somewhat more widely than from the narrow loophole of personal pleasure and advancement, it is strange how small a portion of his thoughts will be changed or embittered by this proximity of death.

He knows that already, in English counties, the sower follows the ploughman up the face of the field, and the rooks follow the sower; and he knows also that he may not live to go home again and see the corn spring and ripen, and be cut down at last, and brought home with gladness.

The farmers apart, I doubt if anyone in the village experiences gladness when they see a combine and its lone driver at work. But the stubble invites young riders. Harvest opportunists, girls wave as he drives past. Gulls fly in stages over the fields, which have been lightly turned over, crying wildly.

John Constable

NOON. A serene hour. I celebrate it in a garden chair. Intending to pull a fast one on the forecast on the rain, I have been mowing since six – or from very early, at any rate. Yet the sun still shines in open disobedience to what was foretold. Over my head, in the old ash, invisible birds are kicking up a racket. Otherwise, all is silent; although I still have in my head the devouring crackle and roar of Jonathan's yellow monster as it eats its way down the farm track, doubling its width. From a blackberry-bound footpath, it has become a Chaucerian highway.

Jonathan enquires if my and his old houses were built with ships' timbers, and I say that England would have had navies unparalleled to provide all the beams attributed to them. No, looking up as we both did, that wood was cut from the hedgerows and forests. And when it was already centuries old. Now it is iron-wood.

But noon. Mountainous clouds apologize for briefly hiding the noonday sun, and the rain-drenched flowers are doubly scented. Pleasantly aching from my labours, I nurse the lazy white cat.

Were it 200 years ago, John Constable would have walked by on his way to Uncle Abram at Garnon's. There is a riverside pasture there still called Constable's meadow. When the artist made a bid to capture the attention of the Royal Academy with his work – 'my six-footers', as he called his greatest landscapes – he named one of them *Noon*. It showed a wagon having its axles cooled in the Stour at midday. It would become the proto vision of the countryside, *The Hay Wain*. His friend Archdeacon Fisher gave it this title, although the vehicle is more likely to have been a timber wagon than a hay cart. Such a vehicle would have carried the oak beams to my and Jonathan's farm sites.

While the Royal Academy remained tepid and near-blind about Constable's work, it was praised in Paris, where it laid the foundations of Impressionism. Almost the only recognition of it here was by *The Examiner*, which thought that it 'approaches nearer the actual look of nature than any modern landscape whatever'. Which is why, as somebody remarked, *The Hay Wain* is now the English countryside of every English mind.

Would the artist's *Noon* have been a better title? It has all the listlessness of midday: its reverie of summer heat, flies, and drinking horses, of not much more to do. Of the wagoner calling it a day. I spent my boyhood by such water, wading in a bit, bare toes squeezing the mud. It provided my first sense of ennui. The smell of the river remained until bedtime. It held the torpor of the valley in July, signing it off on my skin with insect bites. How amazing to have been able to paint all this.

Constable sold *The Hay Wain*, *The View on the Stour*, and another picture, to a dealer for 250 guineas. Recently, another of his six-footers, *The Lock*, sold for £20 million. But today's art prices have more to do with investment than painting, with having somewhere to put one's money. Somewhere safer than the banks. Constable told Fisher how worried he was that the mockery of critics would injure his children. They played by this pool.

The Most Beautiful Nonconformist Chapel?

AND from Anglican matins to East Anglian Nonconformity at Walpole Old Chapel on a burning Sunday afternoon. The cornfields sizzle, and the familiar scenes hurry by.

I mount the pulpit to talk about John Bunyan. We sing 'He who would valiant be' with Tony at the harmonium, if not lifting the roof, elevating our faith. The River Blyth flows out of sight; the graveyard is feathery and unmown.

The chapel was built a decade or so after Bunyan's death, and it remains a perfect architectural response to what remains of our inbred Nonconformity. Beginning as a Tudor house, it was stripped out and simplified for God.

There will be tea and cakes – 'This was the Queen Mother's favourite sponge.' I wander about the burial ground. 'And here they all are,' Nina, the poet, writes.

Samuel Stopher, Mary Stopher,
Timothy Sparrow.
All gone, come to full stops
Of stone.

When I was a boy, there was a lending library where I could borrow Baroness Orczy's *Scarlet Pimpernel* novels for tuppence a time. It was a kind of corner shop, with immense timbers, and part of an ancient house where Bunyan had stayed when he came to give the Suffolk Dissenters a piece of his mind.

He was an impressive figure: large, commanding, muscular from humping an anvil about, and strong-voiced from preaching in the fields near Bedford. Had the Church of England not locked him up for this, he would most probably not have written a word. As with St Paul, and a whole host of prison writers, he called for a pen when the key turned in the lock.

I imagined Bunyan in the timbered room, now lined with novels; or tying his horse to a gigantic nail that protruded from the blackened king-post.

A marvellous find at Walpole Old Chapel was David Holmes's *An Inglorious Affair*, which tells of a classic Nonconformist row in Suffolk in the 1870s – something against which the Trollopian quarrel of the Church of England scarcely raised a voice.

It all began with a harvest-tea meeting and an argument about singing the Gloria. A youthful organist asked the choir to sing it in the Congregational Chapel; the Baptists cried 'No!' The Congregationalists then kept the Baptists out of the church for ten years. The whole town was up in arms over the Gloria – 'In Halesworth, they talk of nothing else.'

Standing in the scrubbed, pale, and infinitely sane interior of Walpole Old Chapel, with the delicate scent of home-made cake and wildflowers drifting up the pulpit, and with Bunyan filling my head, all I could feel was this perfect summer's day. Also a sense of ownership – that in some way I belonged here, and it belonged to me.

During the seventeenth century, it was taken to Massachusetts, this Puritanism with its arguments and triumphs – there to become native in a different sense.

Once, walking in Cambridge, Massachusetts, with its London plane trees, and its Fogg Museum, containing a roof angel from a Suffolk church, I thought I could smell what I am smelling at this moment: some indefinable odour of place. Particularly when the sun brings it out.

Virginia Woolf

A PENSIVE morning. Adrian is mowing the grass, up and down, round and round. The white cat watches from her wall. The postman crashes along the farm track; the horses gossip on the hill. The brook splashes to the Stour. The sky is colourless. Wild geese flow over in echelon and outriders, whirring away.

The radio becomes alive – somebody is talking about Virginia Woolf, and jogs my brain. The friend who is showing me Sussex slows down, and there, on the left, is Monk's House. Hesitantly, for Leonard Woolf has been dead only a month, we steal through the gate and stare into the window.

A long table and a chair initialled 'VW', half-opened parcels, pot plants wilting, dumpy cretonned chairs, a fadedness such as rooms get when everyone has departed. And nearby is the lane to the river. I thought of Virginia filling her pockets with stones before she reached it.

Her passing has always been summed-up for me by Sidney Keyes, who was killed in the Western Desert:

Over that head, those small distinguished bones
Hurry, young river, guard their privacy;
Too common, by her grave the willow leans
And trails its foliage fittingly.

Except they buried her under the garden elms, and they, too, were dying as we shut the garden gate. Her guests were long gone: Lytton Strachey, Duncan Grant, Morgan Forster, Maynard Keynes, her husband, Leonard, the servants who sang, the whole Bloomsbury nation.

But when I find my copy of *The Waves*, although a stream of press-cuttings pours onto the floor, the novel itself flows on in all its careful beauty. It was a 1947 Christmas present. I re-read a few pages. Surprisingly – I had forgotten – the story begins in Suffolk, but soon wanders up to Virginia's beloved London, each character coming to the front of the stage, as it were, and presenting himself. The writing is spare, yet filled to the brim because of what it suggests.

But it won't do, just after breakfast. Chores await; letters beg replies; the telephone which had broken down has been invisibly mended. Calls come in. Had I forgotten? You were going to tell us about Laurie Lee. Black coffee and dark chocolate. And matins on Sunday for St Matthew.

He was old moneybags in the old windows, a crudely attributed apostle. His was the most despised of all occupations, a Jew who not only collected the Temple tax, but also that which his nation had to pay to the Roman Empire. He had actually purchased the right to collect it. And here was Jesus, associating with such a person. How could he! Even his reply – 'It is the sick who need the doctor' – failed to satisfy them.

And it could not have been welcome to Peter, Andrew, James, and John when the Lord invited Matthew to join the little group, and it would have taken some time for them to accept him, let alone love him. He was 'called' in Chapter 9 of his Gospel. Jesus had been on one of his healing walks and sails, 'and as he passed from thence he saw a man named Matthew sitting at the seat of custom, and he said, "Follow me". And he arose and followed him.'

No giving notice to the Romans. No selling his coveted licence to another would-be publican. No hesitation. 'He arose and followed him.' Matthew and his Gospel and fascinating examples of renewal. Autumn feeds renewal. Decay nourishes life.

OCTOBER

Murmurers and Complainers

THREE muntjacs – two grown-up, one a fawn – are feeding on wet blackberries, 50 yards from the house. When they sleep, do they dream about Java? They eat delicately, taking each sodden fruit at a time. Their red-brown coats are thick and damp. They have oriental eyes and twitching scuts. The white cat surveys them from the woodpile window without indignation. Ash leaves sail down onto their broad backs, one or two settling like poppies on the heads of Albert Hall soldiers.

It is very still. Also warm. The tail end of the Church's year. Harvest-festival flowers hang-on in the cold aisles. It is Simon and Jude. I look them up. Killed in Persia. Poor October men.

I have written '*Finis*' to a book. Put out more flags. I must sharpen my scythe and do something about the orchard. There are badger tracks between the failing horsetail. Also a daily accumulation of pear and oak leaves. Not to mention a muntjac highway.

We have lunch in Willy's pub. Everyone we hope to see there, is there. In a confused world, how wonderful it is to find so many people in their rightful places. I preach about St Cedd, Bishop of the East Saxons, coming down from Lindisfarne to bring light to them that sit in darkness – a young man with yellow hair and a painted book. Very bright. Finding an old fort that once belonged to the Count of the Saxon Shore, he turns its stones into a cathedral. But his congregations meet under

121

oak trees, and, in autumn, leaves tumble down onto their bent heads. They sing hymns that we have forgotten. Maybe here at Bottengoms, when nobody had heard of Java.

My friend Charles Causley's poem was put up in lights on Piccadilly Circus. It was National Poetry Day. It turns everything around: 'I am the song that sings the bird.' He lived in a Cornish house named 2 Cyprus Well, Launceston. How often we went on jaunts from there! I showed him Suffolk; he showed me Cornwall. Only long ago.

'I am the word that speaks the man.' He hated gardening. They said he should have been Poet Laureate, but he would not have liked that, either. He took me to see Sabine Baring-Gould's grave at Lew Trenchard, and I took him to see Edward FitzGerald's grave at Boulge. It was a courteous exchange of sites. Poets are so lucky. Their voices cannot die.

I thought I had better read St Jude. He is ferocious. Oh my goodness! But I like his attack on 'murmurers and complainers', and I love his exulted signing-off. 'Now unto him that is able to keep you from falling, and to present you faultless before the presence of his glory with exceeding joy, to the only wise God our Saviour, be glory and majesty, dominion and power, both now and ever.' Now and ever. That is the thing.

It is now 10 a.m. There will be coffee-breaks in the City. Here, the morning has not decided what to do, but continues to rest in misty indecision. I would sit looking out on it, were I not so disciplined. I must pray for the gift of sloth. No need to do that, the white cat says: 'Take a lesson from me.'

St Jude in his few hundred words is hyperactive. But then, they all are. And never more so than at the turn of the year. Dreaming keeps you busy, of course. And watching muntjacs eat hips. And wondering if we could sing the office hymn for Simon and Jude. But much is beyond us. Especially when late October gets into the church.

Pure Colour at Norwich

ANGELIC days. Two feet of white cat stretch out in the sun. But the first ash leaves sail down, wavering in the air before landing. The grass is soaking wet and ruled with badger trails. Undaunted blackbirds sing as though it is May. It is warm and bright, yet at the same time a little sad. The orchard smells of rotting falls, and I think of Aunt Aggie's triangular orchard and its tall hedges and padlocked gate – a kind of Suffolk Eden after sinful boys had been driven out.

Now and then we would be admitted, led by Aunt with her stick, to find an apple in the dank grass. Wiping it on one bosom, she would give it to us. 'Eat it on the good side, dear.' All the picked apples would be laid out in Eaters and Keepers order in the apple-room to scent her clapboarded cottage out until Christmas at least, when it would reek of home-made wine and cake.

In the village churchyard, a suckling was splitting her gravestone, and moss was devouring her name. All around her Blythe and Allen humps posed problems for the mower. There used to be crab-apples and bullaces in the churchyard hedge. And over it the cries of Acton United on Saturday afternoons. They vied with the rookery.

Peace, peace, the gravestones whispered hopefully. But Bottengoms is comparatively silent in October, that yellow month. And full of flowers: late roses, self-heal all the year round, and summer plants reluctant to call it a day.

The artist John Nash taught me to look at seeds, to value their shapes, to regard them aesthetically as well as horticulturally. Or deadheadedly. 'They are part of the life of the plant, don't forget.' The friend who comes to mow the lawns, when asked what he thought of the garden, said it was 'unusual'.

And never more so when October thins it out, and yet at the same time fills it with senescence. And such warm weather!

As for the churchyard horse-chestnuts, the ones the Victorian priest planted in the 1890s, they celebrated conker time with their usual glossy panache.

The conkers lie in their exquisite casings like Fabergé jewels. I put a few in my pocket after matins for old times' sake. I think of boastful 'tenners' and 'twentiers', long ago.

To this day, I carry a conker scar on the palm of my right hand: I was skewering it when it skewered me. Our churchyard horse-chestnuts are a wonder. The village would not be the same were they felled. 'Lift up your hearts! Life up ye conker trees!' And the rooks agree.

To Norwich Cathedral to see the new windows. No glassy saints but their realm of pure colour. Visit them at once if you are in Norfolk. John McLean, who made them, reminds us that colour is the most emotive aspect of church windows, but it was George Herbert's lesson,

A man that looks on glass,
On it may stay his eye;
Or if he pleaseth, through it pass,
And then the heaven espy

that continues to teach us how to approach them, and never more so than this pure-colour addition to religious art. 'I feel I had permission for the quadrants of colour tumbling across the design,' the artist says.

One thinks of Matisse, and then of so many things that one would not have thought of in a Norman cathedral before. Stunning, captivating, loaded with prayer colour.

Secret Observers

THIS week, the lectionary says, we remember Thomas Traherne. But who, once introduced to him, could forget him? They call him the master of the affirmative way. Lost for centuries, he famously turned up in one of those second-hand bookshops, having been through every kind of fate to make him non-existent, including burning.

But there it was; a Mr Brooke found him, charred, but still so starry that he was thought to be Henry Vaughan – 'My soul, there is a country far beyond the stars.' Vaughan and Traherne were Welsh-border people, near neighbours in time, who gloried in the holiness of children. Once a year or so, I travel through their territory to see my friend Edward Storey, who dwells – who is perched – on Offa's Dyke.

The view from my old house is one of exclusion by hills. I dwell in a leafy bowl, and in great quietness. Except when the badgers are about. Last October, Patrick Barkham sat up in a tree to watch them. Although he wore two jerseys, two windcheaters, and a woolly hat, he pretty near froze to death, but all in the science of badger-watching.

We spoke of the historic fear of the dark. Badgers come out just pre-darkness. I had told him: 'Everything changes at night. The trees change. Even places you know backwards take on another life at night. They become mysterious. I don't find it fearful, but there is a history of people finding it fearful.'

Years ago, I had forbidden the local hunt to draw my wood, chiefly so as not to frighten my badgers. The aspens I planted there now reach for the sky. And the badgers have made lanes in the grass to the brook; a grumpy progress at dusk. The brook feeds the Stour, and is glitteringly clear. The white cat, as well as the wild animals, drinks from it, her face tipping the water.

According to Patrick's book *Badgerlands*, I had told him that I was acquainted with the night. Which indeed I am.

I love the story of the cautious Nicodemus, in St John's Gospel, who took care to come to Christ by night. After all, he was a member of the Sanhedrin, not some local fisherman, and too important to be seen with this unofficial person. There is a rare portrait of him in the east window of St Michael's at Discoed, the man who took his reputation in his hands in spite of creeping through the dark streets. What did they talk about? It was the necessity of rebirth.

It was during this furtive conversation that Jesus said, alarmingly and wonderfully: 'For God so loved the world that he gave his only begotten Son, that whosoever believeth in him should not perish, but have everlasting life.'

After the death of Jesus, Nicodemus came out, as we say. He 'brought a mixture of myrrh and aloes, about an hundredweight', to wind into the shroud, when Joseph of Arimathea gave the poor body his own grave, and thus, in a series of Welsh border thoughts, the October day brings me from East Anglia to a Welsh shepherds' church. A subdued light is the norm there, but not here. A fine rain falls.

What shall I talk about in church on Trinity 19? Badgers and Counsellors? Are we to sing Lamentations? It says so in the book. 'Mine eye runneth down with water, because the comforter that should relieve my soul is far from me . . .'

Fiery Furnace

WHEN I was a child, I marvelled that the cows and horses did not jump over the fence and trot off to Bedfordshire. I had found Bedfordshire on the map, and it was clearly as far as anyone could go. When I grew up, I walked *The Pilgrim's Progress* through it, this allegory signposted all the way.

'What keeps you hanging around the house?' I ask the white cat. 'Is it greed, or love?' She gives me a look of beautiful obscurity. Yet the horses on the hill, their legs soaked to the fetlocks by the heavy May rains, do appear unadventurous, just munching and conversing, timelessly.

The old shack by the horse-pond having been removed, the

once wisp of a quince which it hid comes out in all its porcelain perfection. Merial sees it as she parks the car. The artist John Nash would have planted it, possibly to have one of its scented fruits handy for the dashboard. I return to its blossom later, then study its pedigree in my wonderful *Hooker's Finest Fruits*, the Debrett of orchards.

It is the pear-shaped quince, *Cydonia oblonga*, and it made its way here from the Tower of London, where Edward I planted it in 1275. Long before this, it wandered from Turkestan to Crete, to Athens, to Rome, utterly delectable all the way, and a lesson to us all. Chaffinches hop about in its black branches. William Hooker painted its portrait, and our great-great-grandmothers 'quickened' a pear-pie with it. Some dead fruit, black as witches, from last year, dangle amid the blossom to provide a lesson of sorts.

At matins, we listened to a tale of ruler insanity as Nebuchadnezzar stoked-up the fiery furnace for Shadrach, Meshach, and Abednego wearing 'their trousers, their shirts, and their hats', and we sang 'Brother, sister, let me help you', and I read the banns for Emma and her tall husband-to-be, whose name has fallen out of my head.

The Book of Daniel is full of the most amazing stories, my favourite being the banquet and the writing on the wall. It is operatic, with a full cast and stunning scenery. This will tell madmen not to meddle with Jews! Hitler should have read it. It is barbaric and saintly all at once. Daniel, dreaming on his bed through three reigns, created it. But not as long ago as was once thought. Only St Mark quotes from it in the New Testament – 'the abomination of desolation'. The fiery furnace flames up in the Benedicite, and in the imagination of Benjamin Britten; also in the Marian persecutions of the Reformation.

Some of the best radio ever, *Shakespeare's Restless World*, was recently presented by the director of the British Museum, Neil MacGregor. I am writing this in a room that existed when

Shakespeare was writing his plays. The broadcasts have been furnishing it – but also, alas, emptying it with their dreadful accounts of the 1603 plague. Lonely farms were not crowded cities, though, and could have existed untouched, like the 'fever hospital' for the small Suffolk town that stood in the wilds when I was a boy.

We have a clapboard 'pest-house' in the village, built in the 1603 plague year, and still called the black house, although now it is snowy white. The brilliance of the *Shakespeare's Restless World* talks was the way in which they connected us with our common past.

St Luke's Little Summer

A GOLDEN day for St Luke, one of my heroes. I talk about him at matins to a thin-on-the-ground congregation. Luke, the New Testament's Renaissance man, doctor of body and soul, artist, travel writer – everything. Also the birthday saint of the Greek-English boy who lives up the road, and who, at the moment, is choosing which university to apply to.

It is Luke's 'little summer'. The garden, while fading, is burning into life. I am reading Colm Tóibín's *The Master* for the second time, sitting in the garden and nursing the white cat. Ash leaves sail down on us. An unseen farm vehicle clatters behind my wood. The postman bumps down the track. Birds sing as best they can, their soloist fled to Africa.

Among Luke's qualifications, he was a physician of the soul. Think of being able to put this on one's CV. He wrote both his Gospel and the Acts of the Apostles in demotic Greek – the language they spoke in the market-place. But he was astute, taking them to 'the most excellent Theophilus', presumably a publisher.

I like to think of Theophilus unravelling them: first, the

adventures and words of the Redeemer; then a marvellous traveller's tale as Christ's life and words were sent on their journey.

Luke's biography is plainly written. He never married; he was Paul's young helper; he wrote his Gospel in Greece; and, some believed, he walked to Emmaus with the Lord after the crucifixion for the first holy communion. He – Jesus – would have gone on but for that hospitable 'The day is far spent.'

'Lighten our darkness,' I say. Was Thomas Cranmer referring to the brightness/blackness of the Reformation? Or was he thinking of what *Veni, Creator Spiritus* describes as 'the dullness of our blinded sight'? These questions arise after my having returned from my ten-yearly visit to the optician to have my glasses renewed. The optician is in his twenties. He stares into my eyes with a torch: 'Look left, look right, look up, look down. Read as far as you can. Choose your frames.'

I feel that he should have complimented me for being able to see at all, let alone see some of his letters. But he is there to give sight, not praise. His own eyes are child-bright. He is reading a very long novel, he says. I know the feeling.

I go to Marks & Spencer's and buy fruit, snowy underwear, a voluminous dressing-gown, and much else. I feel sensible and extravagant. I walk past the wall which the Romans built when St Paul and St Luke were tramping from Antioch. The traffic is climbing round it like insects: the packed school buses, the commuting cars. A medieval church clings to it for dear life.

Flags fly. Students hump homework. A young man takes out a trumpet and his friends fall about laughing. When the music is unexpectedly fine, they lapse into an admiring silence. On the way home, the taxi driver tells me: 'You're the first today.' I tell him that I am sorry. 'Don't be sorry,' he says.

I spare him the muddy farmtrack. There are sloes and hips in the tall hedge. The white cat meets me part of the way, not too pleased with my absence. The harvest is sugar-beet, the wheat having gone what seems like a lifetime ago. Little streams feed the river – the Stour, which John Constable painted all his life, and mostly in London; for we take our native places with us wherever we land-up.

I don't need new spectacles for these old scenes. I peer at the cat through them, and she winks back. I read Tóibín through them. Can he be any brighter?

NOVEMBER

'I am Michael's Bell'

EVERY morning, between six and seven, I meditate on the view from the kitchen window. That is, I drink tea in an armchair, staring at the view across Duncan's meadow, there being nothing else to look at. Birds, chiefly seagulls, whirl around. I suppose not that long ago, and at this particular time of the year, a holy looker might consider them to be the souls of the righteous.

In church, I will read the long list of the departed, and this does create a strange sadness. Can so many have gone to God, and so soon? And their houses gone to others? Their chattels, too? What a curious name for one's furniture. It rattles like a box.

Last year, peering through the local depository, I saw up for sale the pretty chairs that belonged to an old friend. The ones on which we sat at lunch – a long drawn-out affair because, having got us to her cottage, she could not bear to let us go before four. The gulls leave nothing behind other than a cry. They should be eating the horses' leftovers, but they wing on currents, Chinese-white against the still-vivid autumn green.

I gather fallen pears from the dank grass, wash them, halve them, bake them with just a mite of sugar. And a clove or two. As patron of a nearby redundant church, I should go to see the Christmas lights switched on, but a gale whips up.

The aspens rage, and loose branches fly around. The vine

131

clings to the south wall for dear life. This year, it has paid clinging calls on the *Garrya*, an ash, and a climbing rose. It isn't at all cold, but benign, if uproarious. And, so as not to appear defeated by weather, quite a lot of people come to church.

A neighbour fetches her daughter from a party at Buxhall, where you can read one of the earliest bell-ringers' ciphers: –12345–21345–23145–23415–23451 . . . About 1620, shall we say? Until then, there was just a merry clanging or a sad tolling. Engraved on a bell not far from there, in Latin, is my favourite inscription: 'Box of sweet honey, I am Michael's bell.'

'Can I take our bell-ringers' service?' Brian enquires. They have made me an honorary ringer, although I have never done anything more than some emergency tolling. Not for me the Buxhall arithmetic. But we can't all be brilliant.

But I preached on Dr Luke without a note, he being a favourite apostle and the Renaissance man of the New Testament – which doesn't mention autumn. Only summer and winter. And spring only once.

Ezekiel mentions a vine that withers 'in all the leaves of her spring'. A bad sign. A problem for *Gardeners' Question Time*. A problem for me is pulling all the branches out of the farm track. I find jobs like this more meditative than staring out of the window at the birds.

Ever since I was a boy, I have been fascinated by the imaginative benefits of hard labour – although David's chainsaw is a help. It whines in the shortening afternoon, gives little screams. Flames dance in the wood burner. Advent looms, and keeps me on my toes.

My track begins deep in a sloe and hawthorn enclosure where the little owls have dwelt from time immemorial. Worn to a flint groove between tall banks, it becomes the bed of a tiny river when it pours. Gathering strength as it passes the house, it runs into deep ditches, and soon into the Stour. Tom's Lincoln cows eye it morosely.

'The poor crooked scythe and spade'

TWO blackbirds gorge on berries below the study window.
They stand a yard apart, eating and balancing. But no fruit in
the orchard for me. Not an apple, not a plum. And the wheat
harvest is way down, and were we living in Thomas Hardy's
day we would be saying the prayer 'In the time of Dearth and
Famine'. 'And grant that the scarcity and dearth, which we
do now most justly suffer for our iniquity, may through thy
goodness be mercifully turned into cheapness and plenty.' But
it was the summer rain, not my iniquity which did it.

In John Donne's Holy Sonnets, he remembers:

All whom war, dearth, age, agues, tyrannies,
Despair, law, chance, hath slain . . .

Dearth is dearness. I no longer know the price of anything
– butter, eggs, pyjamas, bacon, the cinema. And now this
harvest's bread. I buy three loaves, and put two in the deep-
freeze. A charming soil-tester comes and tells me what I have
never been told before about our village fields, stones and all.

At the optician, a young man asks me to read A Z L M O,
etc. 'Try the next line.' In the High Street – the same down
which the Romans wandered – the young and old make their
way. I buy next year's Gardener's Diary. How efficient I am.

Changed and in my toiler's rags, I prepare the orchard
for the scythe. Everything must lie low. E'er the winter storms
begin. I am the great leveller. I think of Oliver Cromwell, of
harvest supper, of the last chapter – how to begin it. In church, I
must remember not to mention St Luke's little summer, so that
people do not exchange looks and give little smiles. 'Wait for it
– he will tell us that it is St Luke's little summer.' But what shall
I say instead? Shall I leave dearth alone?

The farmers and their wives pray. As do the Waitrose

customers. All bowed. Honeybees, fruit and veg, the token sheaf, the rich scent. The sun on the painted saints, on the Lord himself.

'I can't bear it,' the old friend used to say as she watched market-day from her car. Meaning that it would all go on when she was 'gone'. The stalls, the schoolchildren on the bus, the swing-doors of the shops, the town-hall flag, the plane flying low, the people chatting, the church clock striking, the girl laughing at the counter, the lovers holding hands, the October air. Everything would go on. She couldn't bear it.

Three labourers have spaded their way down to where the Romans trod, raising a mountain of blond rubble. People look down on them. A wit: 'Have you lost something, mate?' On they dig. I take a short cut through long Victorian roads, which are named after Cromwellian generals, and get lost. Most of my short cuts are a long way round. Surprisingly, a villa calls itself a Russian Orthodox church. What a squeeze it must be. Incense and icons in the front room. Rich responses climbing the stairs.

And now, home. What shall we sing on Sunday morning? Do we know 'Light of the minds that know him'? It is a prayer of St Augustine of Hippo, and is about our treading out our own Emmaus road. A little rain falls.

At the War Memorial

REMEMBRANCE Sunday. The old chaps – I include myself – come to sing 'I vow to thee, my country'. The church aches with Georgian sadness. Medals glitter. Memory holds the door. In the pulpit, I repeat myself unashamedly; for we all like to sing and hear what we have heard and sung before. The November day, too, is carefully unoriginal. I doubt if anyone present can put a face to the names on the war memorial.

Jesus was against looking back: 'Remember Lot's wife!'

And, beautifully: 'The light is with you for a little longer. Walk while you have the light, lest the darkness overtake you; he who walks in darkness does not know where he goes.'

The victims of the First World War certainly hadn't a clue where they were going, Father included, a teenager at Gallipoli. From a Suffolk farm – to this! He stares at me from the piano, a boy who had never heard the news; for the *East Anglian Daily Times* merely added to the mystery.

I say the names on the war memorial yet once more. Then mount the pulpit to read the whole of 'They shall grow not old as we that are left grow old'. Laurence Binyon wrote it almost before anyone had been killed, in September 1914. He was a middle-aged librarian who would have been amazed to know that a verse from his poem would be quoted in every church in Britain once a year. Later, we all fill the pub, glad to be alive. Conkers glisten in the churchyard grass.

The Westminster Abbey librarian Laurence Tanner once showed me the letters from George V about burying an unknown soldier just inside the great west door. And what a business it was to find a spot that had not been buried in before. The Great War will soon be a century ago. Re–reading Ted Hughes's translation of *Beowulf*, I thought that, although war should not become poetry, it does. And none more so than the Great War, in which millions lost their one and only life.

Mark's Gospel describes Christ's almost logical acceptance of war: 'When you hear of wars and rumours of wars, do not be alarmed; this must take place, but the end is not yet. For nation will rise against nation, and kingdom against kingdom . . .'

But I am alarmed at what seems to be a human realistic acceptance of, say, the trenches to come. On Remembrance Sunday they are bathed in the lovely language. Their disgrace is silenced by poetry and music.

This year, we have the added reminiscence of real Paul Nash trees, the recent gale having lopped off branches along the lane.

Wind-torn trees look as wounded as shelled trees. Splintered boughs are uncannily like fractured bones. Chainsaws whine in the distance, one while we sing Isaac Watts's 'O God, our help in ages past', that perfect commentary on Time.

I put the garden straight, pick grapes, pick up pears, chide the white cat for watching me through a window and never in all her life doing a stroke, and breathe in the nice rottenness of autumn.

I suppose the young labourers on the First World War memorial must have tramped to Bottengoms to tidy-up after a storm. So many hands then. So few shillings. And one of the same pear trees. And endless sticks and logs for the fire. And the cool stream running to the river on and on without a break. Constant movement, endless stillness. And those brief lives on the war memorial . . .

Early 'Orisons

ROUND about 6 a.m., should you be calling, you will find the white cat and me at our matins. The sun will soon be up and gathering strength, and it will send a golden line along the rim of Duncan's field. This, at all times of day, is as far as I can see.

I am reminded of the commendatory prayer, 'Life is eternal; and love is immortal; and death is only a horizon; and a horizon is nothing save the limit of our sight.' An oak that was no more than a twig when I came here is a fine tree which catches the morning blaze. What a business it must have been, ploughing up to the horizon. Not a sign now of all this toil. Just autumn grass and the perpetual munch, the dawn appearing, the day's work ahead.

No point in clearing-up after the gale until all the orange leaves are down. A rose – Duke of Wellington – is in full flower. The new lectionary has not arrived; so I don't quite know what season it is. 'You are cut-off down there,' an old chap says. True. All this early brilliance, and not knowing the time. You have to walk a mile to see the church clock. It is golden like the sun. Barry keeps it in order.

Now and then, I have to wait until it has told the time before announcing the first hymn. 'Good morning on a lovely day. Let us begin our worship with "Jesu, the very thought of thee"', which is Barry's favourite. Mrs Cardy's was Addison's 'When all thy mercies, O my God'. And off we go.

I think of Sir John Tavener and his Russian Orthodox music. We arrive; he leaves. The dawn breaks. The nights pull-in. Georgians sleep on the north, we on the south. And somewhere lie the ploughmen who topped my horizon, turned around, and followed the rut to my house. This, donkey's years before they fixed a clock to the tower.

A fine fuchsia (*Fuchsia magellanica* – 'drop tree') is a flourish of bells by my front door. The first frost will see them off. I have to take the annual bell-ringers' service – this is famous ringing country. 'Have you put it in your diary?' Yes, yes. Our ringers are great travellers, driving to Cornwall, Edinburgh, you name it. They are non-parochial and without horizons. 'We rang in Liverpool last Tuesday.' Really? So, what with the commuters and the ringers, I am the permanent stay-at-home, the man below the hill who at this moment is being showered with turning leaves, acorns, and dead wood.

It is Benjamin Britten's 100th birthday. He would have been walking the marshes as usual, staring ahead, passing the yacht club, seeing the boats being wintered out of the corner of his eye. And then leaving the earth at much the same age as Tavener. Last autumn, I gathered maple leaves from his grave.

Aldeburgh will soon be wild, the North Sea flinging the shingle about, the dog walkers putting a brave face on the wind. They call it 'getting a breather'. Sheltered in my river valley, I call it 'before Advent'. The grapevine hangs in tatters, and on to anything it can get its tendrils on. And everywhere there is this turning, turning, this dying colour, this packing-up of the summer. The poet John Clare described it so well.

> With sudden stir the startled forest sings
> Winter's returning song – cloud races cloud,
> And the horizon throws away its shroud

Like me, he is betimes to find some length in the shortening days.

Crossing the Ford

ALL HALLOWS. A furtive sun, a drift of, mercifully, unblemished ash-leaves. They sail across the study window, semi-shrivelled and blotched like old hands. But the rose *John Clare* flowers, and a yucca promises to, any minute now. Which is unwise of it. The season is both lively and deathly. Winter wheat is ruled across the fields down by the Stour. And, to maintain the geographic pattern, echelons of geese fly over the old roof as regular as clockwork.

My old farmer neighbour, a Framlingham boy, has died. His sons are into onions in a big way. Strings of them, red and white, dangle in my larder. Enough to last a year. I have taken the tender plants in from the frost, scythed the orchard, and am about to tidy-up, in a fashion. For nothing approaching neatness will be accomplished until after Christmas. At the moment 'The King of Glory passes on his way.'

James, from the University, arrives, to confess that he does not write letters. He emails. Sloth, of course. He devours cake. Never? He shakes his head, and I shake mine. I point to two shelves of *Letters* in my library, and there he is, a professor, without a letter to his name. A succession of visitors make their

138

way down the muddy track, and are granted audience. The white cat sits on them in turn, dribbling with joy. The village is pensive. The surface of the lanes shines. The hedges are machine-cut to within an inch of their lives. They are what is called a parallel universe.

But the water beneath the bridge swirls about any old how on the surface, though with deep, dark thoughts. Another fall, another bitter time to come. This is where Widermund kept the ford. I see him as one of those St Christopher young men, splashing across shallow rivers with dace and carp swimming between his legs. He would have waded a dozen steps from Suffolk to Essex, heard the watermill, witnessed the kingfisher. 'Do you keep a diary?' I ask the letterless teacher. He shakes his head. 'Through gates of pearl streams in the countless host.'

Ladies appear to sell me a poppy. People on the telly wear them weeks before Remembrance Sunday. Why is this? It seems more to do with respectability than with mourning.

Last Sunday, I preached on Amos, a hero of mine. An unlicensed preacher, this young fruit-farmer from Tekoa had the nerve to 'lift his voice'. He lifted it against liturgy and contentment, and against national happiness. God said: 'Prophesy unto my people.'

'He showed me a basket of summer fruit and said: "Amos, what do you see?" And I said: "A basket of summer fruit." And God said: "The end is come upon my people."' We hear the sadness in his voice.

Summer fruit ends the orchard year. Only this year, there was no fruit. Not a pear, not a plum. I imagined Amos and God in the sycamore-fig orchard. A burst of October wind rattled my trees. Now and then, civilization begins to crumble, and an unprofessional person says what has to be done. And those in power say: 'Who gives him leave to speak?'

God tells his orchardman, 'I will smite the winter house with the summer house . . . I will not hear the melody of your viols . . . I despise your feast days.' This was too much for the high priest. He told Amos to go where he couldn't hear him and prophesy there. Minor prophets can be a trial, especially when they write so well.

'They shall grow not old'

LOVELY but sad days. The leaves fall, the sun shines, in church we muster for the Remembrance. It has become a kind of saints-day, filling the aisles with its devotees. We turn to its memorial, and I say its liturgy. Its words are by the librarian-poet Laurence Binyon, and were published in *The Times* long before the Western Front massacres had begun. 'They shall grow not old, as we that are left grow old.'

As a boy, I used to think that these soldiers would have found this cold comfort, and would have very much liked to have enjoyed a long life. But their melancholy suits the Georgian language of the Remembrance. We sing Isaac Watts's 'O God, our help in ages past'. Charlotte Brontë has a girl, 'her voice sweet and silver clear', sing it in *Shirley*. Our voices, though darkened by time, do justice to this masterpiece. And so the service goes on, inside and outside. I preach on poppies, botanical and symbolical, blood-coloured and bloody.

It was the Jewish poet Isaac Rosenberg in 'Break of Day in the Trenches' who released, as it were, our emblematic poppy, the one we button-hole. A rat touches his hand 'As I pull the parapet's poppy to stick behind my ear'.

Flanders was traditional farmland. Corn and its wild flowers had grown alongside there for centuries. Just as its birds sang above the din, so did its poppies bleed in its mud. The imagery seems to grow more intensely every Remembrance, and my sermons ever more botanical.

But our greatest time-hymn, 'O God, our help in ages past',

says more and more to me about mortality and immortality. Or so I find. It is grand, sonorous, truthful, accepting, tragic yet comforting, and it first appeared in Wesley's *Psalms and Hymns* in 1738. A poignant verse was left out long ago, but it uncannily suggests the Western Front:

> Like flowery fields the nations stand
> Pleased with the morning light:
> The flowers beneath the mower's hand
> Lie withering ere 'tis night.

Too far to walk, we drive from our church to a steel memorial by the side of the road. It is to the American airmen who came to Wormingford on St Andrew's Day in 1943. Some 200 of them were killed – too many names to read out and halt the Sunday traffic racing by. Their colonel, almost a hundred, sends a message from the United States.

My father, a teenager at Gallipoli, refused to attend these rites, the band playing, the mayor in his robes, the snowy war memorial in the little Suffolk town. Once central, it has long been put at the side of the road so as not to delay a flood of cars. Otherwise you would have taken your life in your hands.

I say Binyon's words all over again. They float in the mild air. I remember my friend John Nash, who painted both the trenches and the Second World War docks, and Christine, his wife, who ran a canteen at Portsmouth for the sailors. John told me that 1939 never meant as much to him as 1914. His brother Paul painted the Battle of Britain, the Heinkels and Spitfires like stars in the Kent sky. And so it continues, the reality and the dream.

Between services, I rake-up fallen leaves, mostly from the giant oaks which stare out of the valley into the next parish. They are all in line, their roots in the everlasting stream, their tops spying Little Horkesley.

Dust into Dust

THE rival claims of Leicester and York to Richard III's bones – as a tourist draw, one cannot avoid thinking – do not mention his dust. Dust has never been collectable. Yet it is dust that remains when all else is gone. Shakespeare's own epitaph famously deals with both dust and bones.

A long time ago, I was leaning over the brass communion rail in Stratford-upon-Avon church, intoxicated by the nearness of this peerless dust, when I was told off by the verger for hurring on it. 'Excuse me, Sir, but don't hurr on the brass.' A reasonable request, when he had just Brassoed it. He then confessed to having left West Bergholt, the village next to Wormingford, to live in Warwickshire – 'Because my wife couldn't stand the way the brambles hung out of the hedges.'

Shakespeare, back home after a less than respectable career on the London stage, had almost certainly turfed out the occupants of a fine tomb in his parish church in order to make a place for his bones. And cursed be he who moves them. All this, not in the hand of one who had written the sonnets, but in threatening doggerel. Above him, Sunday after Sunday, the living hands took the living bread.

A different dust, and a different tomb caught my fancy at this time: that of the poet Edward FitzGerald. His gravestone put the blame for his oddness on his God. 'It is he that hath made us and not we ourselves.' It spread a little lopsidedly in the dank grass. Maidenhair and dog-daisies blew over it in May.

Being a dreamy young man, I often joined them. And this is where the mortal dust came in. And from far Persia, not Suffolk. I knew *The Rubáiyát of Omar Khayyám* by heart – a sceptical masterpiece. Wry and sadly happy, it says: seize the moment – seize it from the moment you wake to the moment you die. Jesus said much the same thing. Don't look back.

Remember Lot's wife. Live today. And then comes the Persian dust in the English churchyard, just down the lane from me.

> Ah, make the most of what we yet may spend,
> Before we too into the dust descend;
> Dust into dust, and under dust, to lie,
> Sans wine, sans song, sans singer, and – sans End!

As everyone was talking about Benjamin Britten being a hundred years old on the feast of St Cecilia, I remembered his telling me about living in Snape mill, and how his piano was ebony black when he went to bed, and dusty white when he came down in the morning. Generations of flour had filtered down from the beams. It pleased him.

Ancient dust is in permanent free-fall in my farmhouse, which is as dry as a bone. Dusty seekers are setting out for Bethlehem, crossing deserts, looking up, and with a long way to go. No sooner do I put a foot into the church than it is: 'Don't forget the Advent carol service . . . the bell-ringers' carol service . . . the Nine Lessons.' Do not forget a thing. Do not forget the dusty feet of Palestine. Do not forget 'the Lord will come and not be slow, his footsteps cannot err . . . Truth from the earth, like to a flower, shall bud and blossom then.'

What a strange time it is, this Advent of Christ. So ordinary, yet so mysterious; such a setting out, such an arrival. 'Ah, what a dusty answer gets the soul When hot for certainties in this our life!'

DECEMBER

Bare Altars

AN EARLY December afternoon, with slanting sunlight. The feast of Nicholas Ferrar, to be exact. Does he have a feast? So he left Little Gidding in Advent. Thinking of him, I see such a sun drawing long shadows from a group of elms that Vikram Seth and I noticed growing there. In a circle, but too close together.

Two horses on my meadow crop the muddy grass, and will soon be moved on. The sky is pink and yellow. Now and then, a handful of starlings pass in full flight. A few miles away, in both directions, high streets will be crowded with shoppers and plangent with canned carols. The white cat dozes among geraniums.

Girls call out from polished horses. 'It is coming!' we shout – not Christmas, but the storm. Only it often misses its way, in spite of the forecasters' directions.

I take a funeral, and prepare two Nine Lessons and Carols. Winter is all departures and arrivals. The former is back to front as usual, the cremation preceding the service. An old friend, now with God, wanted ten hymns.

'You can only have three.'

'Oh, very well.'

A relation from the other side of the world would talk about her with tears. No flowers in church. And the Second Coming pushed to the back of our minds.

And the sweet scent of trampled grass, and the squabbling rooks in the near-naked trees. But youthful winter wheat in all

directions, and the river is high. It tugs at the iron bridge that
ties Essex to Suffolk, where the Saxon ford would have been.
'No heavy traffic.'

A summer boat has been hauled up, and lies meditatively
in the rushes. Will we have snow? Who knows? 'Don't forget
the bell-ringers' service,' Brian says at the door. 'You don't have
to do anything, just the welcome and blessing.'

He does so much – they all do, and not only here, but in
thousands of parishes. Such music, such words. Only don't rely
on the organ at Mount Bures, which goes up when it should
go down, or something like that. I actually delight when, *in
extremis*, we sing unaccompanied.

We are to think of Samuel Johnson, my boyhood hero.
His statue looks towards Fleet Street from St Clement Danes,
where Mother went to Sunday school. He would walk from
City church to City church, hoping to hear a decent sermon.
But his ears failed him, dear, good man.

His prayers are self-reproving. His virtues were
marvellously Christian. He housed a trying female, fed his cats
on oysters, made a black boy his son, suffered from multiple
aches and disfigurements, and confessed that the ultimate of
human happiness was to ride in a swift carriage with a pretty
woman.

I once carried *Boswell's Life of Doctor Johnson* round the
Hebrides, reading it wherever he went, not so much in his
footsteps as in his complaining shadow. It was early summer,
and I was youthful. It was my first glimpse of Scotland.

Pressed flowers, bog cotton, campion, and heather stain its
pages. May on Skye! Bare feet in the burns. And the telling-off
by my Wee Free landlady for swimming on the sabbath. And in
my ears Dr Johnson's grand put-downs. Poor young Boswell.
I'm not surprised that he got drunk.

But now Advent all over again. The coming of Christ. Its
haunting language. Its bare altars. Its wheeling birds. Its heart-

breaking music. Its fear and its glory. And all those names for Jesus – Adonai, Dayspring of Nations, Emmanuel . . .

Thou Dayspring from on High

WHAT Coleridge called 'the secret ministry of frost' was given early this morning. At 5 a.m., they say. The garden stiffens, the blackbirds catch the crumbs that fall from the blue tits' table. The air is as sharp as a knife. The bare trees creak. The sky scuds about. The postman skids. I burn ash logs.

Keith, who mends the old house, looks for indoor jobs. Christmas is coming. But the High Street is restrained. In the public library, which was built as a corn exchange, a shelterer from the winter blast complains about the modest heating. But the village bus is moderately cosy. My track crackles underfoot. We sing:

O come, thou Dayspring, come and cheer
Our spirits by thine advent here.

Although, as a matter of fact, my spirits are not low. Holy music keeps them high. Advent song is the best of all. It has something to do with its being better to travel hopefully than to arrive (Robert Louis Stevenson). I often include his prayers when I take evensong. He wrote them for his household in Samoa; so I have to translate them to a cold climate. The fresh flowers that his people put in their ears at morning would have been wilting. And that Edinburgh voice – and the fleeting breath! He was forty four when they carried him to the hilltop. He said that every man was his own doctor of divinity, in the last resort. He said that we underrated the duty of being happy.

In an unfrozen afternoon, I do a bit of raking. Rough toil brings the best warmth. Bottengoms is sheltered. At midnight at this time of the year, the stars blaze down on it.

146

Homing planes pretend to be one of them. People are putting on their seat belts, putting their books away, feeling for the ground. My Australian nephew Michael will be looking for business class after bankers' meetings. How he gets about the universe! My house was old before Sydney existed.

I had taken him to where his father and I cycled as boys, to where we climbed Suffolk church towers. 'Come you down, you little varmints!'

All the churches smell the same – a pot-pourri of damp books, lasting flowers, and holy garments. And indefinable 'presences'. Out of season and in season, they are jolly cold. Wooden and marble knights. Last Sunday's hymns on the board. Worn steps. Last Sunday's lessons waiting to be re-read. Philip Larkin's marvellous words to enchant me. And how wonderful to be old and to take no notice of progress. To read the poets and not the theologians. Although one must stay awake in Advent, as St Luke insists. 'Stay awake! I say.' Else one might not hear that Love, the guest, is on the way.

I take in the tender plants, take cuttings, take care not to over-water them, having scrubbed the rustic pots. One or two geraniums are in bloom; so they are given a last scarlet show on the piano. The central heating in the sitting-room has been turned off, and I am surprised that they don't freeze. The pictures stare coldly from their icy frames. I fetch the winter curtains from the cleaners. What else? Stay warm! I read Elizabeth Bowen's stories. Old friends for December. And thank God that you have not inherited an Irish country house.

Churchmen – and Churchwomen

THE tremendous Scottish gale is 'noises off' as I write. It is roaring over Leargan, where we have sat, read, talked, and rested many a summer. It will be hooting down its chimneys, crashing

147

through the plantations, and bringing down deadwood in piles. Here, at Bottengoms, it is but the faintest tail-end of its strength. Just enough wind to bowl the oak leaves over the grass.

Picking up the post from our fine new box in the orchard – to save Jamie's steps – I see primroses in flower. Not that this *braggadocio* on their part will stop the winter. It is mild and rough. Rooks blow about, ditchwater gathers strength. The white cat is a cosy breathing ball in the old dairy where the lawnmower lives. 'Call me in April.'

The funeral of an old choir-friend in a full church. I hear her singing voice as I say a prayer about her and music. Everywhere, these faithful singers, and at all times. Dear souls who know their Merbecke from their Advent anthems, who ring bells, robe, hold the worship together. What a space she leaves, what a silence.

Earlier this month, we celebrated the feast of St Ambrose, the singing Bishop of Milan. A fourth-century judge, he was offered his see before he had been baptized. Didn't George Herbert go to Bemerton before he was wholly in holy orders? Another singer, if you like. But it was Bishop Ambrose who demanded congregational singing, not just choir singing. The Church itself must lift up its voice, as in *Songs of Praise*.

Sometimes, watching the latter, and all this complex religious doctrine set to music, I do wonder what is happening. Probably no more than the blissful act of singing itself. The youthful TV choirmaster goes to schools where boys and girls have never sung. How strange this is, and how have educationists allowed this to happen? Huge establishments without a song? Ambrose would have been nonplussed. I am nonplussed.

I hear the enviable voice of a schoolfriend in the great Suffolk wool church soaring in the solo, our Welsh rector with his head aslant in professional appreciation. The Early Church sang Ambrose's *Splendor paternae gloriae* – 'O Jesus, Lord of heavenly grace' – every Monday morning, it is said.

Ambrose is the father of church music in Latin Christianity. Lost at the Reformation, it was discovered again by the Victorian translators.

St Augustine listened to Ambrose's hymns: 'How greatly did I weep in thy hymns and canticles, deeply moved by the voices of your sweet-speaking church.'

They said that Ambrose had a style that was peculiar to himself, clear, sweet, vigorous, grand . . . without glitter, but bright and calm, severe yet enthusiastic. Arians – a sect who denied the divinity of Christ – accused Ambrose of bewitching Christians with his music.

I am easily seduced by church music, now and then losing my place when I am taking the service and coming to with a jolt. Last Sunday, the whole of matins tumbled out of my Prayer Book on to the floor, and had to be taped back in as soon as I returned home.

And now for Nine Lessons and Carols, begun at Truro, Ambrosianly raised to the heights at Cambridge. But sung pretty well by us at Wormingford.

Brickwork

THE morning after the PCC is delectable. Sun-pierced river-mist with the gold breaking through. I see it from my bedroom window, and with a new proprietary air; for have I not this week been made patron of the Dedham Vale Society? Who would have thought it?

But the pre-Christmas scene is indecisive, with trees floating about, and neighbours' houses only half present. Mild isn't the word. 'We shall pay for this,' an old chap says. What with? I rake up the last sodden leaves. Not a bird singing. The white cat asleep until April, the first cards toppling about on the piano, the shopping list hanging out of a book.

We held the PCC in the pub, with the agenda and the menu in tune with each other. The big question, as always, was the wall. What now seems generations ago, the churchyard wall, exhausted by having to keep in the dead, gave up. Thus PCC after PCC it has dominated our affairs. One day it will stand, mended and perfect, and then what will we do?

And the cherry tree, too, has given up. Trees die, we die, walls tumble down. Think of Jericho. Bodging used to be the answer. Better than handing over good money to experts. My ancient house is witness to the bodger's hand. 'Who on earth mended that?' I ask myself. Only to remember it was me, donkey's years ago.

Two Nine Lessons and Carols have to be sung in neighbouring churches. One after the other in the late afternoon. It may not be exactly King's College, Cambridge, but it is breath-taking, all the same. The darkening church, the tremulous first verse at the door, the whiff of mulled wine, the full pews. 'Once in royal David's city' first appeared in Mrs Alexander's *Hymns for Little Children*, and the service itself first appeared in Truro Cathedral. It holds its haunting quality, and continues to cast its spell.

How is it that something so repeatedly sung, done, or said can remain spellbinding? Fragments, mere wisps of liturgy, hang about in our hearts and cannot be excised by unbelief. Familiarity itself becomes unfamiliar. There is no knowing what is happening. Poets know not to grapple with it. To let it be.

My old friend Richard Mabey has given me his selection of Richard Jefferies' writings, knowing how I love his work. There is a passage in it that repeats a passage in my life when the ancient house in which I was born burnt down. This was some years after we had left it. I once took Richard to see it.

Jefferies wrote: 'Such old-fashioned cottages are practically built around the chimney; the chimney is the firm nucleus of solid masonry or brickwork, about which the low walls of rubble are clustered. When such a cottage is burned down, the chimney is nearly always the only thing that remains, and against the chimney it is built up again.'

But my birthplace was never built up. There it stood, for years and years – as I once said, like a great charred tooth – until a smart bungalow dismissed it to history.

I would have been three or four when we moved. All I can remember was the night a wild swan came down the chimney and beat about the papered bedroom in terror, creating havoc, they said. My parents' shouts remain in my ears like an equal terror.

The house was thatched, and birds and rats slept in its roof. No country person had a dwelling all to himself then. The youthful John Clare and his wife, Patty, made love in their company.

In the great space above me at this moment, unwed farm labourers had their bothy: beds of straw, elm pegs for smocks, dormers fore and aft, now lined with bricks, which would have given great views of the Stour Valley. They went to bed by 'a pair of stairs', then by ladder. Elm floorboards ran 'bushes' into their bare feet. Their bathroom was the cold stream which ran through the kitchen floor for convenience.

An immense stone sink, in which the children were scrubbed, contains my late geraniums, now tempting the frost. When the Cambridge people arrived to list my house, they said it was *c.*1600, but economically rebuilt with the timbers of the previous structure, wood from the late Middle Ages. It would have heard the earliest carols.

Now, it hears carols from King's Chapel, Cambridge, and, because he was born a hundred years ago, Britten's Christmas music.

The white cat turns over on a bookcase and says: 'Let me know when it is spring.' But I stay awake, as faith demands. I watch the light failing, the dead leaves clinging to the panes, the horses in quiet conversation in the field, the cards tottering on the shelf, the marker in a novel, the larder groaning, the postman at the door – 'Somebody loves you, my holly hedge shining.'

The cherry by the church gate will not see another December. Lopped, propped, it must go. Whether the dizzy rooks are celebrating or mourning, it is impossible to tell. They whirl and cry amid stars and planes, disturbed by bells. I have supper by ash-light, the furniture glimmering. 'Just like the old days,' murmurs the cat, the squirrels running the length of the roof, the gulls whitening the furrows.

With the December days so warm, it is hard to believe that there will be at least one snowdrift ahead. The dip in the track will be topped up. The ponds will blacken. Some trees will bear more than they can take, and shatter. Winds will take off, the entire village will rattle, commuters will stay at home. Hearths will hiss.

Before and after Christmas are two very different times. Christmas itself, in spite of high spending and dense sociability, has moments of pure happiness and silence. Or a sublimity which must not be missed in the uproar. How to find it – that is the question. It is likely to be as much in the High Street as in an old farmhouse; in a family-packed room as in a chancel. It comes and goes like firelight – and all that preparation! And wrapping paper 'up to here'. As the poor mad poet Christopher Smart said:

> Where is this stupendous stranger?
> prophets, shepherds, kings, advise:
> lead me to my Master's manger
> Show me where my Saviour lies.
> Under Christmas? Hidden by it?

Framlingham, Suffolk

MURKY warm December days. Strangely pleasant. We drive to Framlingham on the spur of the moment. The little town, with its great history, is still and wet. I remember once coming home from baking Sydney, and loving the raindrops sliding down the plane windows at Heathrow.

Advent is in the air: an almost tangible time when we 'put on the armour of light' – an enchanting activity – and when 'love is the fulfilling of the law'. The car splashes past endless empty fields, which are faintly ruled with sugar beet. Framlingham Castle, with its thirteen towers, has an ephemeral look, as though it might blow away, and Framlingham School comes and goes on the horizon, as though telling us, 'Don't take me for granted.'

It was built to educate the sons of Suffolk farmers with money left over from building the Crystal Palace. This sensible idea came from the Prince Consort, whose statue presides in the distance.

We make for the Crown, and have lunch by the fire. Inertia reigns. The old room is full of ghosts: neighbours from long ago; schoolmasters taking a break; my friend the poet James Turner, who vanished to Cornwall; the Falstaffian rector in his cassock, tweeds, and tennis clothes; and my bike in the courtyard.

It was at Framlingham Castle that Mary Tudor learned of the death of her half-brother, Edward VI, and the accession of poor Lady Jane Grey to the throne. Vast events in a quiet countryside. And now a handful of folk in a bar, and the Christmas decorations.

My favourite reason for coming to Framlingham, however, is to marvel yet again at the glorious tombs of the Dukes of Norfolk, especially the one with its Genesis frieze – a favourite of Benjamin Britten, and from which he took his church parable *Noye's Fludde*. He was fascinated, as I was, by the extraordinary things that filled our local churches, and, should one be a composer or a writer, were there for the taking. He would drive off in his big old car on the spur of the moment, as I had done this week, to look once again at what he regarded as his by right of birth: some view, some object in a vast or tiny village church.

But Advent. The liturgy trembles with expectation and dread, with joy and fear. The Creator enters his creation as a child. Advent from *Adventus*, coming. The liturgical year begins. Long ago, it was as severely kept as Lent. But, now, shopping shouts it down. Some scenes on television of bargain hunters were little less than disgusting.

For me, music expresses it far more than words. Music in which Jesus is given such beautiful names: Emmanuel, Desire of Nations, Wisdom from on High, Dayspring, Lord of David's Key, names filled with urgency and longing. George Herbert added to the list: 'Come, my Way, my Truth, my Life . . . Come, my Light, my Feast, my Strength . . . Come, my Joy, my Love, my Heart.'

I rake the main paths, and push barrow-loads of sodden leaves out of sight. Robins fly ahead. Keith arrives. May he take some holly? It is berry-less, but shining, an immense wall of it glittering and clattering when the wind gets into it. Geoffrey Grigson said that working holly into Christian belief was easy. It was thorny and blood-coloured. People once believed that the Cross was made from it. In old ballads, Holly is the man, and Ivy the woman.

But I prefer to see it as it is: evergreen, ever present in the farmhouse garden, and stuck behind the pictures on Christmas Eve.